BUILDING CHARACTER

BUILDING CHARACTER

TRANSFORMING OLD HOMES FOR MODERN LIVING

images
Publishing

CONTENTS

CONNECTED LIVING

THINKING MINIMALLY

A GROWING FAMILY

TIMELESS TRANSFORMATION

PREFACE

Old houses are an integral part of our modern cities and their preservation is an important aspect of architecture. In the world of architecture, we often hear about old buildings that are at risk of being lost forever, due to their defective condition. In some cases, the existing structure is in too poor a state to be retained or restored, or the prospective restoration costs are too prohibitive to allow for renovation, and the building is either demolished for safety, or left to continue its deterioration.

Old homes come in many forms—as varied as the plethora of architectural designs of previous centuries—from an old worker's cottage with limited detail to a midcentury modern house or a classic New York townhouse. An older building can be viewed as a response to its history, carrying the marks from the different cultural, social, historical, political, and economic environments over the years. The best way to retain these old houses for future generations is to intervene with some modifications and additions to bring it up to contemporary standards while still retaining their historic character.

Restoration, and indeed renovation, is the action or process of accurately revealing, recovering, or representing the state of an old building as it appeared at a particular period in its history, while protecting its heritage value. Restoration work may be performed to reverse decay, or alterations made to the building. This might also require some new work, which should be analyzed through the design process prior to adding any new material and/or changes. Some projects require an understanding of its existing context and how it sits in its setting alongside its neighbors.

Such projects are not simple, as unknown issues may be discovered during the renovation process which need to be dealt with prior to continuing the work. The challenges of upgrading an old house to meet modern standards and requirements are plentiful. New wiring might be needed to make it compatible with the new information and communication technology, or the installation of a heating and cooling system, installation of an effective fire detection system, solar power, upgrading the building insulation to conform with modern standards, and so forth.

Most architects and/or designers who undertake restoration or renovation projects on old historical buildings find the process interesting, as there are always personal stories to discover under the layers, in addition to being presented with interesting challenges. The work, whether it's a new addition to an existing building or repurposing a salvaged object or piece of material, adds another chapter and value to the existing story of the house. The attraction of blending new architecture with the old is how the new addition interacts within the overall context of the building.

A good renovation of an old house is one that is sympathetic to the existing building and its historic context, and inserts new work or makes changes that enhance and complement the historic values of the home. This may be done through the adoption of a more traditional approach or the exploration of a more contemporary solution. A deliberate balance between the past and present can create a functional and yet totally relaxed renovated old house.

Renovation work to an older period home can easily escalate into a significant modification and indeed extension. In many renovations, the condition of the old home no longer meets the demands of today's modern lifestyle. Either the rooms are too small or too dark; the spaces are too segmented and not connected; the interior is outdated and deteriorated through a lack of maintenance; or there is no connection with the outside world; or poor ventilation and heat circulation has resulted in rising damp, and so on. By definition, a period house usually consists of small segregated rooms whereas modern occupants crave larger and more well-lit spaces to accommodate their growing family and provide greater flexibility of the use of interior space. Architects often choose to add a skylight in the roof during a renovation, which helps to solve issues with the lack of natural light.

Many old houses have also been muddled by decades of ad-hoc alterations which were done with poor quality construction and materials by previous occupants. Often architects and designers discover original materials during demolition that were hidden by the previous renovation. These original materials, such as an original Travertine or timber flooring, can be revealed (or reinstated) and brought to life again to emphasize the journey from the old to the new. Architects will often employ different materials and finishes to distinguish the new addition from the original.

In times gone by, there was no real indoor-outdoor living element when the old house was first constructed. A frequent request, therefore, is for the creation of a living space that can extend outdoors, bringing the outdoors into the internal living space. Some of the projects that follow show that different approaches can be adopted in order to connect the inside with the outside. Introducing a large opening on a solid wall immediately creates a visual connection between the separated rooms. A flexible opening system such as bi-fold doors that can give an extension to a space when it is needed, and full-height doors, for example, allow natural light to penetrate between rooms.

Another element that is often used as an anchor when linking the internal spaces between the original and the new part of the house is the kitchen. This is an important element as most of the family activities or entertaining happen around this area. It connects the interior and exterior spaces, and allows for easy interaction with and supervision of children.

There are challenges when it comes to connecting and blending a new element with the past. But new additions and old existing architecture can complement each other's uniqueness when the new addition is well designed, and successfully integrated onto the existing historical structure. Such successful renovations are very much associated with respect for the past while continuing to convey the story of human activity and development for the future.

Santoso Budiman, Principal of SWG Studio, Australia

INTRODUCTION

As the modern world changes and evolves, so does our modern lifestyle. Our level of comfort, desire, and overall satisfaction with life is defined in new ways, contrasting to the previous and now surpassed traditional world. We now thrive to own more things, live simpler lives, and reside in open-plan homes. As changes develop, traditional homes are no longer able to satisfy our contemporary needs of living.

The contemporary lifestyle, when compared to the past, is filled with objects that are intended to fulfill our needs and wants, but eventually are forced into storage when they are outdated. Our homes are stocked with more kitchen appliances than we could ever need, more furniture, bigger television screens, and, of course, a car in the garage. Sometimes, there is even a storage room filled with our now forgotten but still needed purchases.

Though traditional homes are no longer able to satisfy our contemporary needs of living, they still have great emotional connections and historical value, whether it is on a personal or public level. Because of this, there is great value in holding onto these buildings, and restoring and redesigning them rather than jumping to demolition and rebuilding. This book follows these ideas through projects which find the bridge between replacement and conservation, creating spaces with historical respect and modern possibilities.

The modern residence today is often generalized in form, space, and interior in order to suit the multiple lifestyles of future occupants. Though this can be seen as a sign of the times and an intelligent investment, the buildings become somewhat temporary to the resident, as well as having a lack of love and warmth in design. Compared to the traditional home, it shows a great lack of inviting features found within the house.

No longer is your place of residence a home in which you will comfortably live the rest of your life and pass it down through the generations. Instead, the home has become merely a house, which will be passed on to the highest bidder. What can be seen of our contemporary lifestyle is lacking the sense of emotional ownership over our buildings. We no longer give the same care that is seen in the presented works into our newly constructed houses. In order to make room for the new, for which we have an overwhelming admiration, whether it is furniture, spaces, or entire homes, we sometimes leave history and tradition behind.

In this publication, architect Max Capocaccia of MC Architecture Studio addresses the idea that we have a desire for change while still holding onto our respect for history in the project Kingswood. He was given the brief from the homeowners to create a personalized home suited to their current lifestyle, with the allowance for interior alteration, and a subtle reflection of the building that stood before it. Due to the 2011 earthquake that struck Christchurch, the previous building's remaining ground floor was reinforced, allowing for the new upper story to take place. Within the building's envelope formed by structurally insulated panels is a vibrant and open space gifting the clients the freedom for the change they admired. The internal walls are non-load bearing in order to be easily dismantled, turning the newly formed spaces into an additional office in the future if their business deems it necessary. The final home was constructed to suit the modern requirements of life for the residents, with a sentimental touch of history surrounding their every day in the reuse and refurbishment of the trusses taken from the previous building. Here, the architect has found the perfect unity between the clients' desires for freedom in spatial arrangement while having a personal connection to a presently fixed home, a tactic that is very present in this publication.

More than 35 renovated homes have been chosen for this publication, for reasons related to variety, inventiveness, and historical value. The image they portray between contemporary lifestyle and traditional architecture is more demanding of attention than any selection of new Modernist-based houses constructed solely as investments. What this book focuses on are the architects who have looked at the original buildings in a new modern light and found inventive ways to preserve them in the modern world. The buildings have been gifted a new life with warmth and connection to the homeowners, either by holding on to personal history with the original building, or respecting and conserving the character of the building.

For example, as seen in the project Valencia House, the clients wished to recover their family home due to its 100-year-old history and personal sentimental value. Therefore, the designer was drawn to maintain the building's attraction while creating a new and more open and functional feel.

With every restoration or renovation project there come problematic issues. Many of the selected projects had issues in the existing layout being unsuitable to modern life, limited storage space, outdated kitchens, and a lack of natural lighting. The project St Vincents Place Residence, as part of a Victorian terrace and thus enclosed on either side by its neighbors, lacked natural light. However, the architect firm B.E. Architecture was able to modernize the home, giving minimal hint from the outside, while creating a modern interior with respect to its original form, thus showing there is always a respectable solution.

Each project comes with its own issues whether they are of structural integrity or a more emotional nature, but they are all addressed with the same care and respect, ensuring that the original essence of the building is not lost, nor held on to too tightly, and restricting the contemporary lifestyle. When done properly, the renovation becomes the bridge between old and new. It must save its history, but also allow for enough change in order to gain the desired modern lifestyle. The creation of a modern lifestyle in an old home is truly the art of balance.

The project Casa Tmolo in Spain follows these ideas in a very direct and prominent way. The two-piece home has been transformed from the remains of an early 1960s farmhouse that had been left untouched for 50 years, leading to its deterioration and overgrown shell of vegetation. The designer has seamlessly molded this deteriorated structure into a lively home with the adaption of existing materials and replacement of unsalvageable structural features. The building's original stonework has been used to express its past in a clear and effective manner while introducing new and respectful materiality coexisting with the history of the building in a contemporary style. A key example of this can be found in the contrasting white concrete facade of the main house, where the white represents the new forms which conjoin seamlessly to the harsh and old stonework. This can be seen as an honest form of architecture. The designer has not tried to reconstruct the previously existing building with falsified and inglorious materials, but rather define the line from old to new, giving more emphasis to the still-standing remains of the building.

Deciding what features of the building should be saved, restored, replaced, or removed can be the defining moment between a well-finished home or a poorly altered mess. Home-defining features with a history or story, whether it is to the homeowner or the public, should always be the first retained where possible. These features then become a form of memorabilia to the loss of the previous structure. This follows the same human patterns where we keep tokens of past friends and relatives in order to remember them or a specific time. These features of memorabilia displayed in this publication vary from large barn-style doors or specific stonework to entire facades or complete shells.

A large difference between the design of traditional and modern homes lies in the use of natural light and openings to the exterior, which may be the street frontage or backyard garden area. Though it is very different between cultures, there is now a larger need for privacy and safety than in previous years. Now we see larger windows and openings to areas of safety, while we hide our homes from the street frontage. This philosophy of safety through privacy is best related back to early Rome, where homes were built inwards, with internal courtyards becoming the main outdoor space, giving the occupants the freedom to be outside without contact or harm from the people of the outside world.

The project House W expresses this theory, subtly protecting the building from the street and opening it up internally, a complete shift from its original form which had poor daylight and posed privacy threats overhanging the tourist busy street. The architects have set each of the floors back to form a buffering space between the privacy of indoor and the publicity of the street frontage. With the use of the semitransparent expanded mesh street-facing facade, the architects were able to create visual boundaries for the occupant's personal security, while still allowing for the much-needed natural light and ventilation. While the facade allows for lighting, internally a light-well becomes the major opening for the home, creating a directional path upwards to the sky following the stairwell from the ground floor to roof, bringing natural light through all levels and rooms. With the removal of partial ceilings, the home opens itself internally also to each of the three levels, prioritizing internal contact and connection over the external street frontage. The architects have turned this 1960s townhouse into a contemporary home adapting our knowledge of history into our modern world.

In my view, history tells us about our journey in humanity and what we learn from it is our key to awareness and progression. While designing for a modern lifestyle from a more recent historical building, the architect must address with a respectful understanding of the current needs of our civilization and community, as well as the building's heritage and generation, taking from it the original goals and achievements for its time, and finally their personal understanding of the journey we have taken through history dating back thousands of years. It is at this point that we can honestly design for a better future, taking the learnings from history rather than the issues or mistakes.

New technology—present in all modern buildings in different ways—has allowed us to evolve and develop in the architectural world. Whether it be electrical, mechanical, or materialistic, our technological advancements have opened vast opportunities and reduced restrictions in our built environment today.

One example in relation to this point is seen in the project Casa VI. The architects wished to continue with the current materiality of the structure—concrete bricks—while building with a modern aesthetic and construction techniques. This allowed for the home to have four equally sized openings to the northern sun, formed with the building's original and locally sourced materials. The architects sought to achieve the greatest possible outcome using materials at hand, such as reinforced concrete, natural larch, iron, and wood.

Technology can be seen in all the featured projects as the large difference from traditional to modern homes. It has allowed for freedom in design and alteration, gifting new life to the old residences while still saving the historical essence.

It is also paramount to address the physical gains on the environment that come from renovating rather than demolishing and rebuilding. The renovation and reuse of existing buildings allow for a large reduction in demolition wastage and material use, defining it as one of the most environmentally responsible forms of design in most, but not all, cases.

For a world currently so heavily focused on climate change, environmental status, recycling and waste, we seem to take safety in the idea that building new and bigger houses is of no implementary loss or negative effect. Rather than jumping directly into this idea of building new, we must first be aware of what we currently have and what it can be transformed into with a little inventiveness and understanding into both its history and desired future. This practice can be seen as the recycling of a building, which recycles the existing materials while also recycling the history and memory of the building by retaining its original essence. In its simplest understanding, much like the reformation of materials at a recycling plant, this is the reformation of an existing building into a new and more desirable home.

As diverse in original form and style as they are, the projects that cover these pages offer a new way of thinking for how we currently build and a solution for living our contemporary lives in old rejuvenated residences. No longer shall we demolish our history due to its inherent incapability to keep up with our ever-evolving modern lifestyle, but rather remold this history in new and inventive ways to progress beyond our modern lifestyle. The image the selected projects portray is one of the contemporary lifestyle in traditional architecture.

Caleb Skene, MC Architecture Studio, New Zealand

CHAPTER 1

CONNECTED LIVING

KING BILL

Located in the vibrant backstreets of Fitzroy, King Bill is the renovation and extension of a double-story terraced house and neighboring garden.

A family of four asked Austin Maynard Architects to design them their 'forever house.' They asked for a renovation to their two-story terrace home, incorporating the empty garden site to the east and reusing the old stable building at the rear. They wanted more living space but they had no intention of maximizing the economic yields by creating a huge home. Instead they sought to give something back to the suburb they love through a rich and generous garden.

Recognizing the importance and heritage significance of the area, as well as the rich eclectic nature of the location, the terrace facade remained untouched. A glazed corridor now runs along the eastern outer wall of the original terrace, linking the old house with the stable (garage and parents' retreat) and the new glass pavilion, which houses the kitchen, living, and dining areas.

At King Bill, the designer set out to completely rethink the terraced house and the principles that created them. Typically, you walk through the front door of a terrace, past two bedrooms to the kitchen/living and small rear yard, which is usually overshadowed by the house itself. The designer set aside these principles and looked at the house as empty spaces that needed new purpose.

Holes were punched through the boundary wall on the east and the entrance was moved to the side to become a light-filled corridor linking the old house with the stable and pavilion. With the entry moved, the original terrace entry porch became a garden and the entry corridor became a bathroom.

DESIGN: Austin Maynard Architects
LOCATION: Melbourne, Australia
AREA: 4,327 square feet (407 square meters)
COMPLETION YEAR: 2018
ORIGINAL BUILDING: 1850s
PHOTOGRAPHY: Derek Swalwell

LA SERENA

The site is located at the end of a quiet cul-de-sac, with fantastic views over the Championship Parkstone Golf Course. Mature maritime pine trees and boundary screening ensured that the site felt a part of the golf course while maintaining optimum privacy.

The original house was a 1970s split level, with a very tight driveway and accommodation over two floors. The clients' brief called for a complete remodel to create a dynamic four-bedroom residence that would tie the various levels together, with an open-plan modern layout interspersed with intimate rooms.

The sloping nature of the site provided an additional challenge, and had a significant influence on the design. On arrival, the house was required to appear as a two-story dwelling. The natural fall in the topography allowed the design to cascade down the slope and evolve into a three-story dwelling, featuring indoor and outdoor living zones opening to a large rear terrace, taking full advantage of the stunning views over the golf course.

The final design ensured a layout that flowed for modern living. On arrival, the large entrance hall spills into the formal lounge, and study, which overlooks the double-volume space. The double-height void in the living area with extensive glazing floods the area with light, extending the boundaries of space, both inside the house and within the environment. Two separate staircases lead either to the top floor master suite and bedrooms or down into the double-volume living space and kitchen. The house revolves around this magnificent large living space, which has a two-story wall of glass facing the garden and golf course.

The house was finished to the highest standards, creating a luxurious, private retreat, with bespoke interior architecture carefully chosen by the architect firm's interiors team. La Serena has been thoughtfully designed to respect the surrounding natural environment. This design epitomizes modern, luxury living, in a stunning, unique setting.

DESIGN: David James Architects & Partners Ltd
LOCATION: Poole, United Kingdom
AREA: 5,281 square feet (491 square meters)
COMPLETION YEAR: 2017
ORIGINAL BUILDING: 1970s
PHOTOGRAPHY: Tom Burn Photography

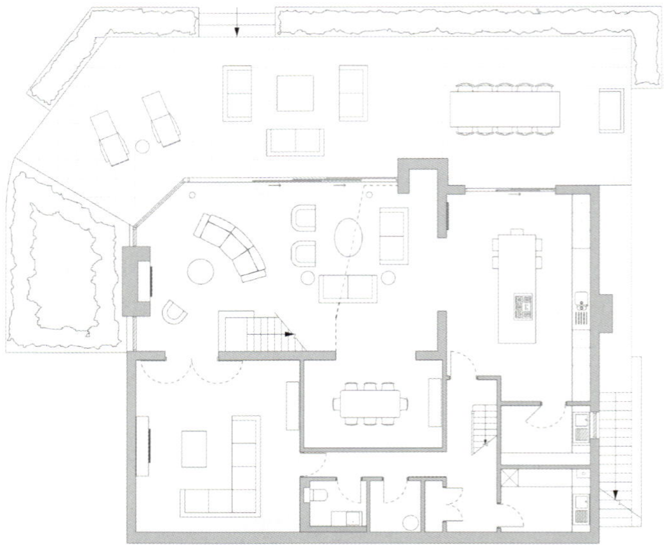

Lower ground-floor plan

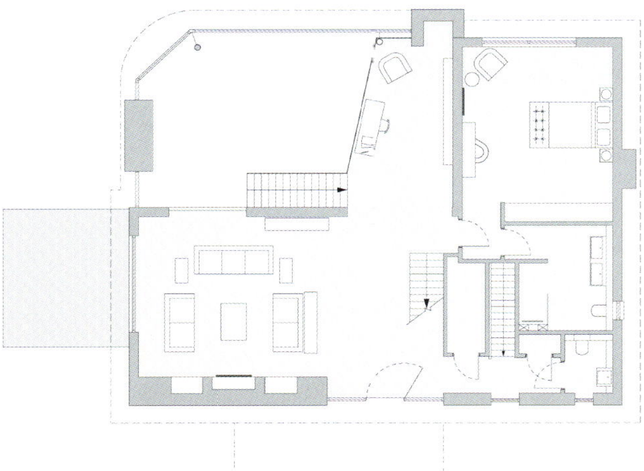

Ground-floor plan

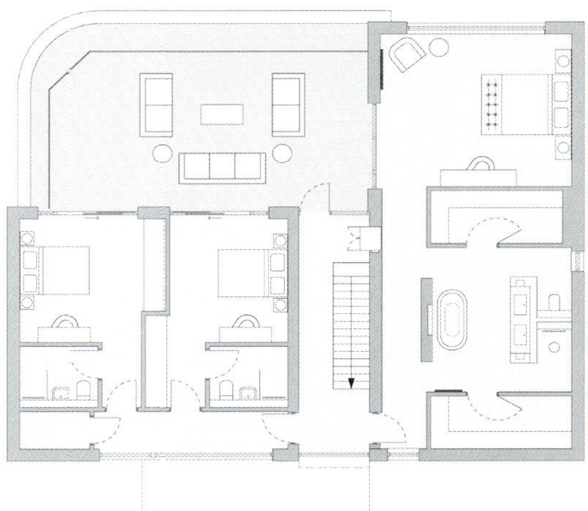

First-flcor plan

CHANEL
CATWALK
KATE MOSS

LAURELHURST MIDCENTURY

The owners, a young family with two children, had recently moved into a midcentury home in the Laurelhurst neighborhood of Seattle. Originally designed by Ibsen Nelsen in 1961, the layout of the home was immediately appealing but the character and flow between spaces wasn't a good fit for the patterns of their daily life. The design task was to renovate the home while respecting its soul and extending its lifespan.

High on the owners' wish list were increased physical and visual connections between rooms and with the outdoors. A central feature of the original design was a courtyard garden, experienced primarily through the living room. Careful reconsideration of the openings surrounding this intimate space reframed it as a tranquil organizing element of the house, central not just to the living room but also to the entry, the daily circulation, and the more informal spaces of the home.

An inviting kitchen with strong connections to other interior and exterior spaces for entertaining and play was vital to the new owners. The original kitchen was walled off from the dining area, isolated from other living spaces, and had limited views and access to the yard. Limited structural changes united these spaces and sliding glass doors expanded the family's activities onto the new deck and patio, framing views of the waterway, Husky Stadium, and the Olympic Mountains beyond. Detailing the casework as freestanding blocks rather than walls allowed the spaces to flow into each other more freely.

While the owners preferred to keep the character of the major hipped roof form, they also wished for improved vertical proportions and increased visibility out of upper level windows. Simplification of minor roof forms around the periphery allowed bedroom window sills to be lowered so children could enjoy the views. Single-pane windows throughout were replaced by modern glazing systems and extended floor to ceiling where needed for a sense of height. Upgraded insulation and a new high-efficiency radiant floor heat system allowed the removal of ductwork and low ceilings, while dramatically reducing the home's energy consumption.

DESIGN: mw|works
LOCATION: Seattle, United States
AREA: 4,420 square feet (441 square meters)
COMPLETION YEAR: 2017
ORIGINAL BUILDING: 1961
PHOTOGRAPHY: Jeremy Bittermann

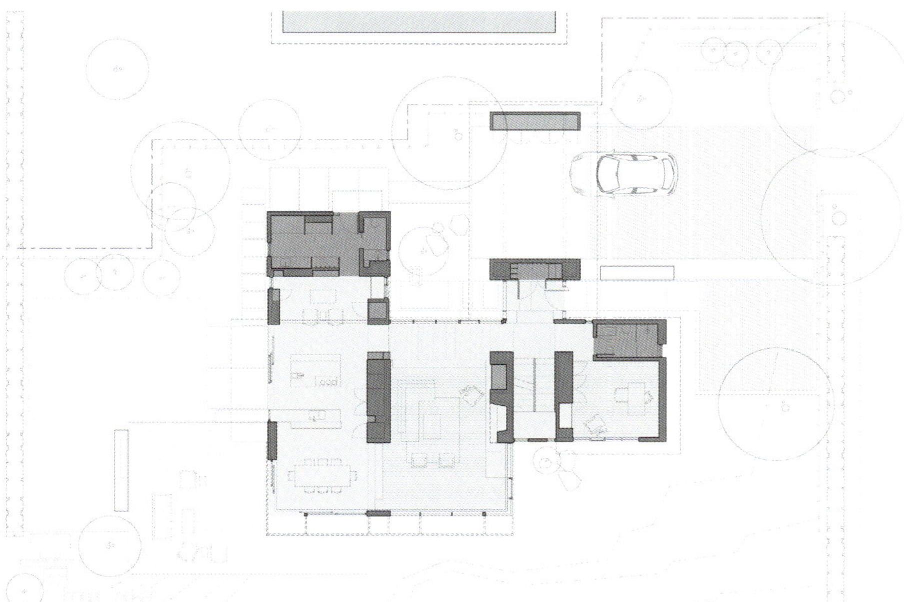

Main floor plan

Miele

HIBOU HOUSE

DESIGN: Barbora Vokac Taylor Architect Inc.
LOCATION: Etobicoke, Canada
AREA: 2,165 square feet (201 square meters)
COMPLETION YEAR: 2017
ORIGINAL BUILDING: 1950s
PHOTOGRAPHY: Scott Norsworthy

This renovation thoughtfully updates an existing traditional 1950s style home for a more modern lifestyle, and allows the house to function as a social 'hub' for a young family that values connection, both with one another and with their friends and neighbors. The result is a home that can accommodate the family's activities, and one that feels relaxed and comfortable yet easily adapted for entertaining.

The layout improves the flow between the spaces in a way that makes the most sense for the desired experience. The resulting space creates a backdrop for the clients' lives and tells a story about the things most important to them: an inviting and inspiring space to entertain, while allowing for plenty of informal, everyday interactions.

Two seemingly contradictory requirements were included in the initial design brief for the project: to create a sense of connection on the ground floor, and to entertain different groups of guests separately—for example, the children could have their friends over while the parents are entertaining.

In response, the strategy was to consider the ground floor as a field with distinct objects located within the larger and now open space: the bar, stair, banquette, and entryway closet. These elements, being more intimate in scale, create smaller alcoves and areas that are still visually connected within the space as a whole.

New dark smoked oak floors work with a modest ceiling height to create a sense of warmth and intimacy within the larger, now open, layout. The custom millwork pieces function as large volumes, defining smaller spaces within the open plan, and custom details are located at key tactile moments, such as the custom flat bar steel handrail and paneled walnut guards.

The new addition—a minimal blackened wood-clad volume—contrasts again with the bright light-filled interior and the large sliding doors and windows at rear of the house open up to maximize views to the garden, creating a strong connection between the interior and exterior livable spaces.

Back elevation

Front elevation

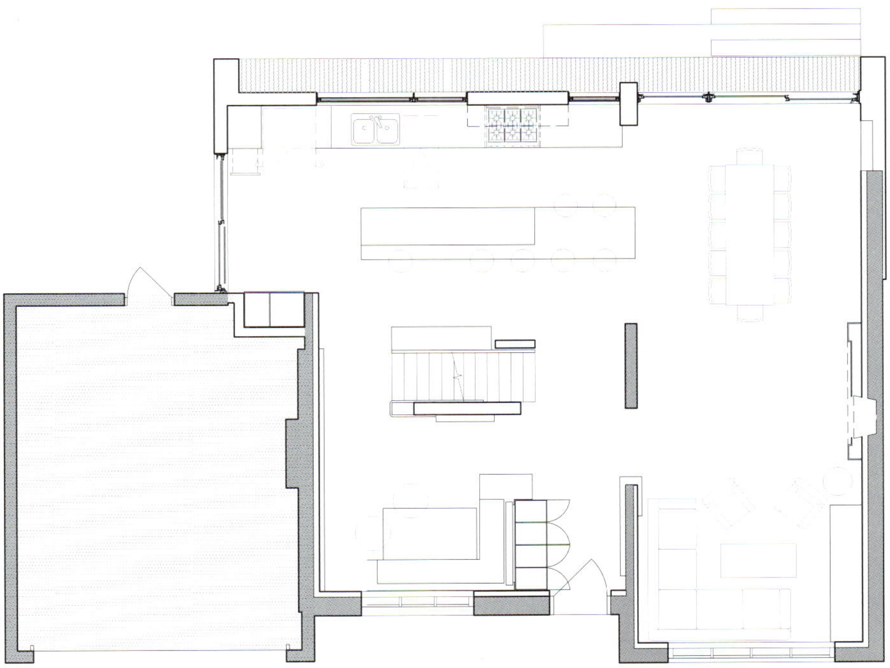

Ground-floor plan

HOUSE W

This 50-year-old townhouse, in a high-density residence area, is a typical Taiwanese design. The main problems for this rectangular-shaped house included poor daylighting, which is common for houses of this specific shape, and the close proximity to neighboring houses, which poses a privacy and security threat. Noises from nearby tourism attractions and night markets were also a nuisance.

To combat the lack of privacy and decent views, the architects decided to design the house inward and upward. The front of each floor was set back to form a buffering semi-outdoor space between the streets and the living spaces, and with use of semitransparent expanded mesh and openings on the facade, the architects were able to set up visual boundaries while still allowing natural light, ventilation, and rain to access the interior. By removing partial ceilings and creating atriums, these semi-outdoor spaces on three floors are linked. The first-floor balcony provides the entryway, with improved natural light; the second-floor balcony offers an extension of the kids' plays area with trees and plants; and the main suite on third floor enjoys green garden views.

Lighting and ventilation were big factors in regard to the well-being of the occupants. By installing large windows at the front and the back and creating an atrium in the middle, sunlight can naturally flow into every corner of the house. The balcony at the back of the house was forfeited and set back so the distance to neighboring houses was expanded. The toilet located at the back uses glass for partitioning to allow as much ambient lighting as possible.

Each floor was created as an open plane with all cabinets located against walls to maximize indoor floor area. White timber floors were used and the walls were given a cement finish. Other materials used include stainless steel, wood, and glass. The white/gray palette offers a traditional feeling, while also helping the reflection of sunlight in the house and the refraction of lights created by the use of glass. The reinforcement of beams and columns was kept without intentional concealing, allowing the existence of both the old structure and new elements to exhibit the unique quality and atmosphere of this renovated old building.

DESIGN: KC Design Studio
LOCATION: Taiwan, China
AREA: 2,131 square feet (198 square meters)
COMPLETION YEAR: 2016
ORIGINAL BUILDING: 1960s
PHOTOGRAPHY: Sam Siew Shien

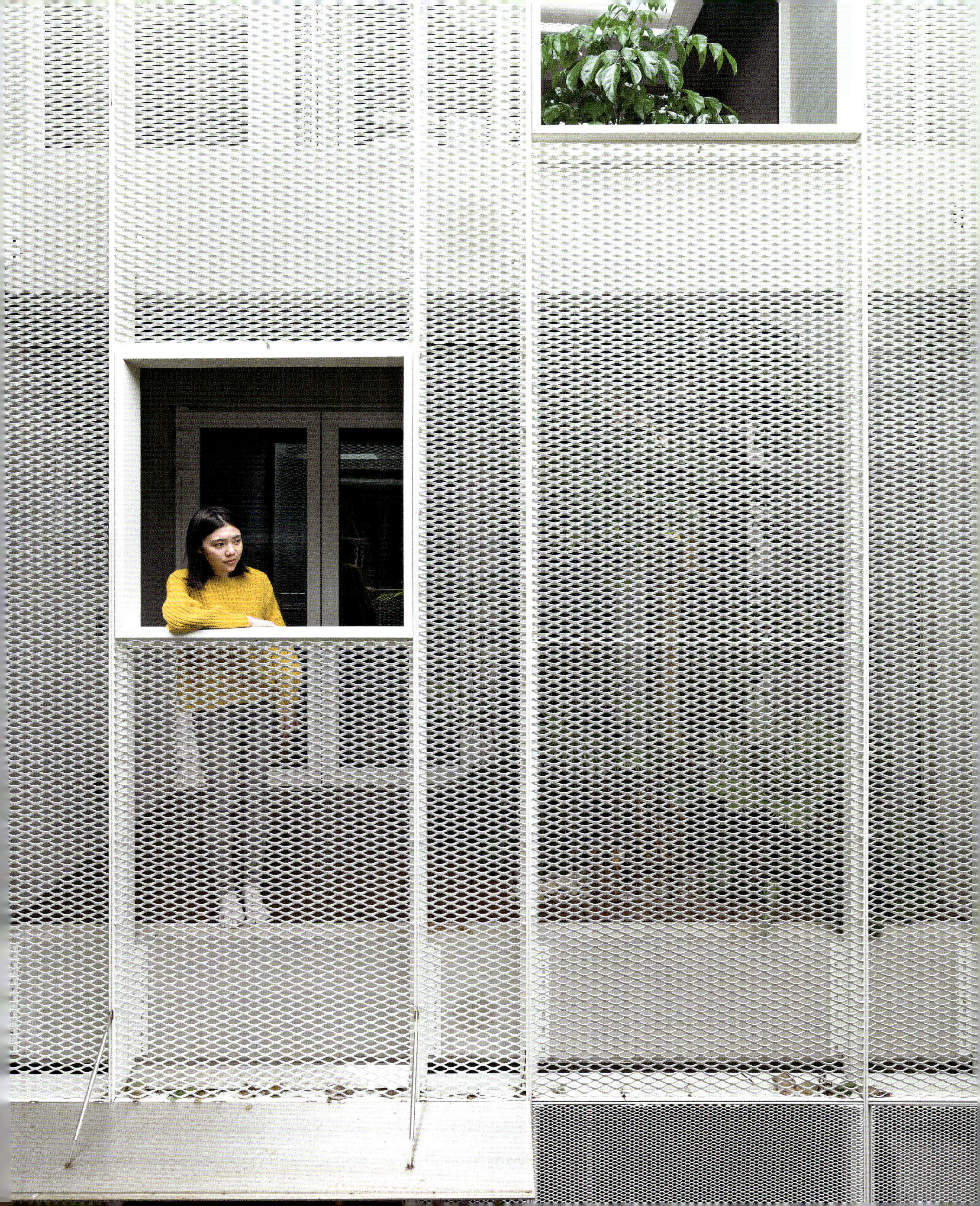

Elevation

Section

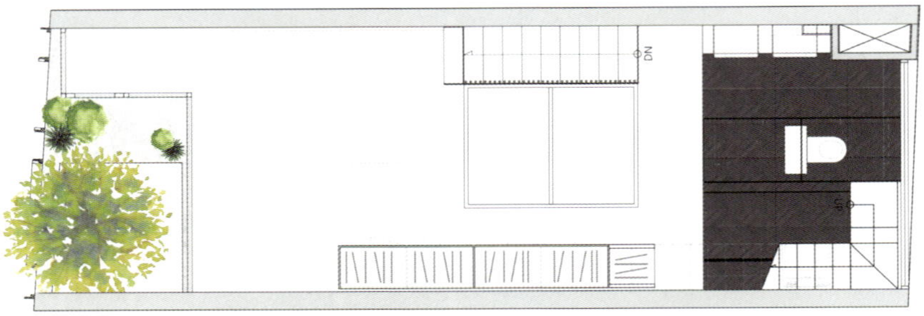

Second-floor plan

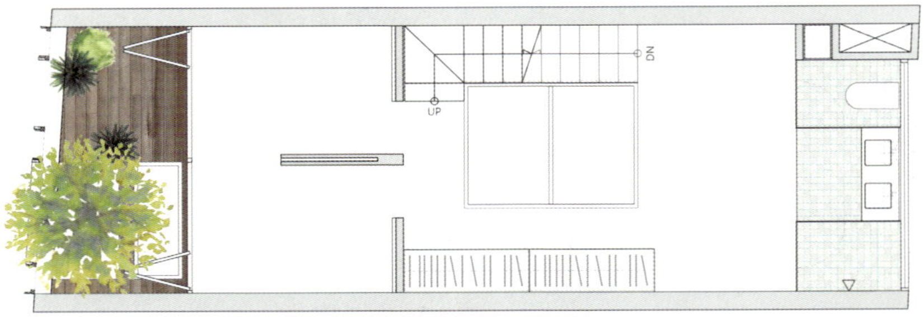

First-floor plan

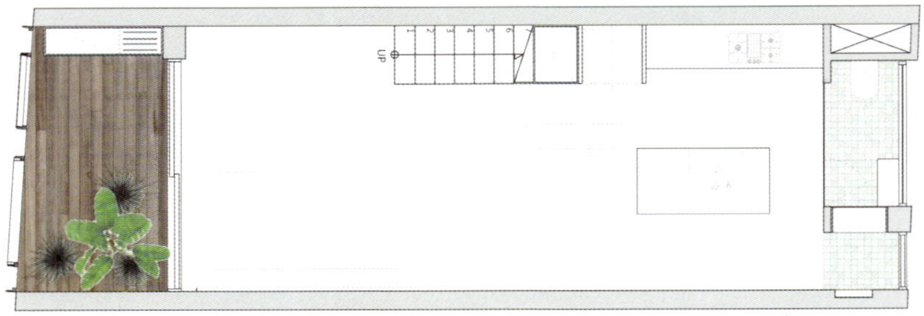

Ground-floor plan

STEALTH HOUSE

The initial brief was to create this home in Sydney's Paddington area to fit the needs of a young growing family, with a seamlessness between the interior and exterior living zones that suits Sydney's balanced climate.

When the client purchased the house, it was in a poor state, suffering at the hands of a bad 1970s makeover, with its historical features having been removed and generally poor planning throughout.

The design intent was to reconfigure the planning so that the primary internal living area directly connected to the backyard, which literally serves as an extension to the living space. The rear yard was made more practical with respect to how it was used. It was previously a sequence of small paved areas separated by changes in ground levels, whereas the new layout attempted to optimize the site's width and open the space up. A new garage was added, with a storage basement below and self-contained guest studio above, bookending the property from the rear service lane.

The street frontage of the three-story terraced house was restored and the surplus space on its western side was reverted from being external to internal—a simple gesture that transformed the entire home, with the result that all of the existing rooms were able to open up to and connect to this thin but tall zone. A new wall that abuts the neighbor's house was built. It is a concrete block wall that serves as structural support within the house, which was then clad with vertical timber planks. This void was given a glazed roof and glazed ends, creating a transparent versus a solid approach that does not compete with the original terrace home. The original side wall of the house was then penetrated to permit access to natural light in the bedrooms, the main staircase, and the bathrooms, creating a skinny three-story void that nearly all the rooms connect into.

DESIGN: MCK Architecture & Interiors, in collaboration with Juicy Design
LOCATION: Sydney, Australia
AREA: 2,530 square feet (235 square meters)
COMPLETION YEAR: 2016
ORIGINAL BUILDING: 1885
PHOTOGRAPHY: Douglas Frost

84

The main staircase is a good example of the void's capacity to bring light into what would otherwise be the darkest space in the home. The staircase is new and it runs perpendicular to its predecessor. Given most terrace homes are deprived in their width, the intent here was to make each level feel as wide as possible, so in turning the staircase 90 degrees, the designer was able to save on the space needed to circulate around a stairs. In this respect, the stair space is almost like a room with no end walls such that moving up through the building the inhabitant literally touches the tall skinny western void.

The designer's philosophy with the glazing was to adopt a black frame, which has the effect of allowing the eye to travel past the frame to something beyond. The result is that interior spaces can feel larger as their apparent boundary is beyond the room's actual footprint. The owners wanted to break the glazing down into smaller panes, which the designer agreed with given the conservation zone. Smaller windows are a distinct characteristic of a lot of the original buildings in the Paddington precinct.

The intent behind the joinery and color palette was to create a neutral palette with large sources of warmth provided through the timber floor and western wall. The black stained joinery in the center of the plan was given a contrasting material to create the illusion that it could be a piece of furniture simply dropped into the home. The reality is that it conceals kitchen functions plus the structural walls required to hold the house up. Deeper into the plan, it becomes the stairs. The floor was fitted with an engineered floorboard made from oak with a limed finish.

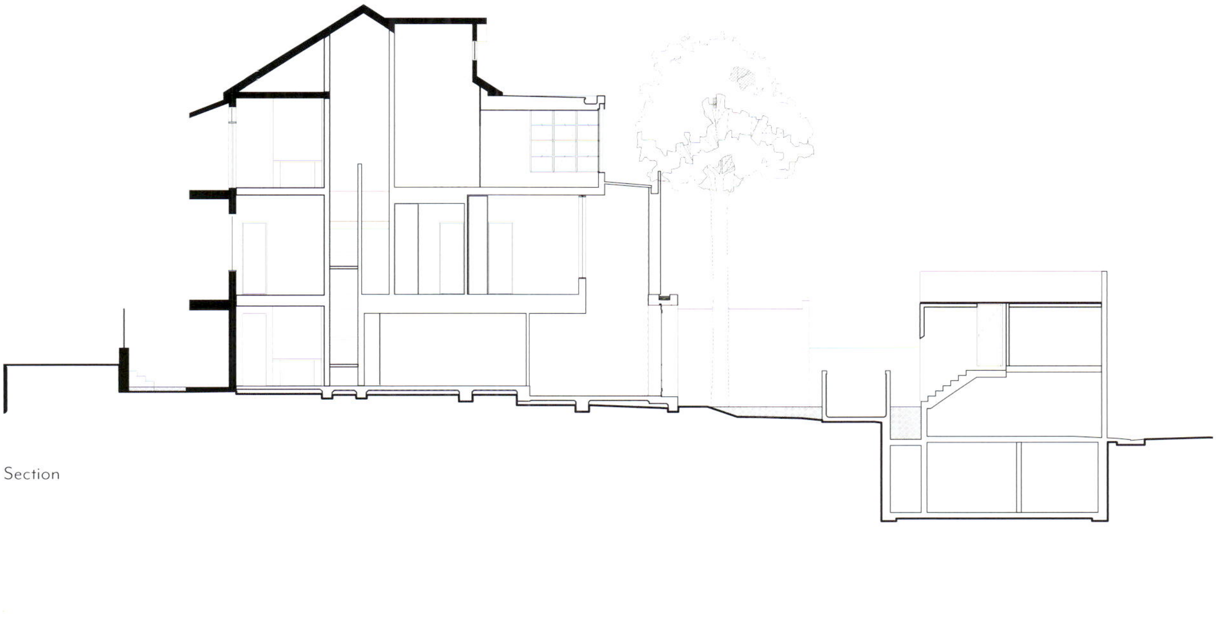

Section

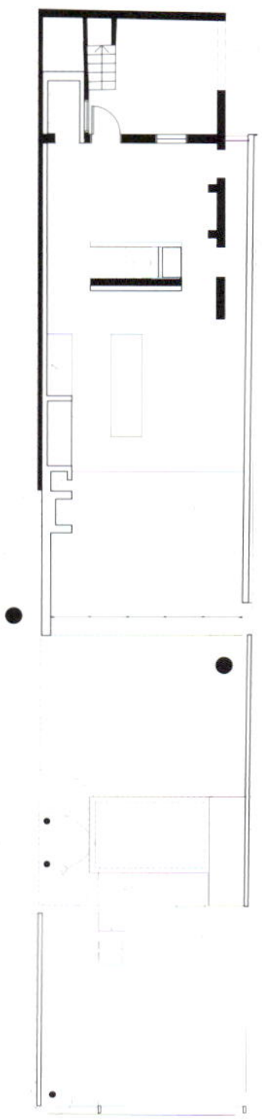

Ground-floor plan

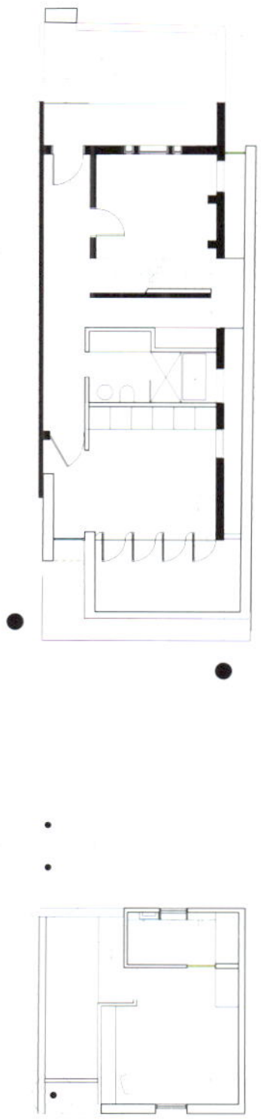

First-floor plan

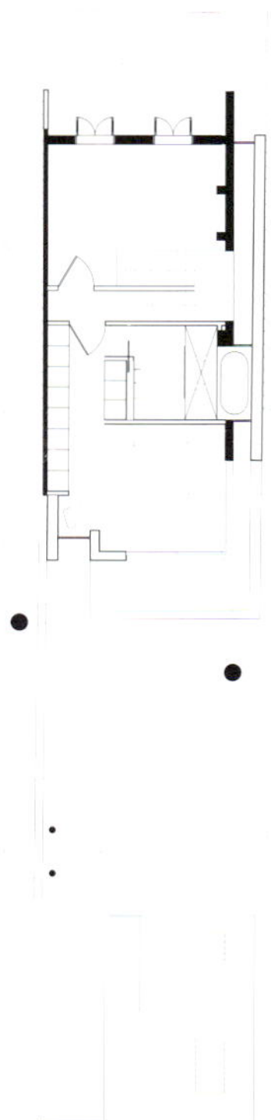

Second-floor plan

23 TERRACE

Situated in the 1970s suburban development of Taman Tun Dr. Ismail, 23 Terrace is a new double-story terraced house reconfigured to replace its single-story predecessor. During the day, the facade is a typical contemporary terraced house with large openings, glass balustrade, and minimalist security door grille and gate. At dusk, the house transforms into a lantern, casting surrealistic shadows on the cement-rendered porch.

It was constructed from the simple architectural principle of 'form follows function' where the needs of the occupants take precedence. On the ground floor, the living room, dining area, and kitchen converge in an open-concept layout, and a suspended split staircase made of steel occupies a minimal part of the living space. The living area has a feature wall of exposed brick, which is one of the few remnants from the old house. The concrete ceiling was left unplastered to reduce VOC emission. A flexible guest/music room with an attached bathroom is accessible via two large panels of folding-sliding doors.

The dry and wet kitchens are connected by a long stretch of marble countertop and stainless-steel cabinets. The centerpiece of the dining and living room is the bespoke dining table carved out of a slab of suar timber cross section.

DESIGN: DRTAN LM Architect
LOCATION: Kuala Lumpur, Malaysia
AREA: 6,950 square feet (645 square meters)
COMPLETION YEAR: 2015
ORIGINAL BUILDING: 1970s
PHOTOGRAPHY: H. Lin Ho

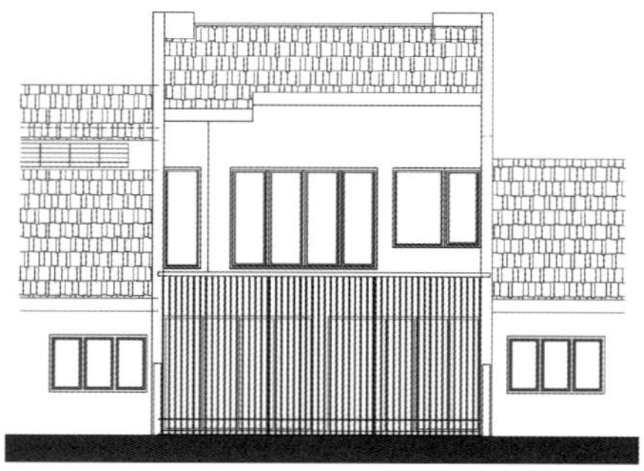

Front elevation

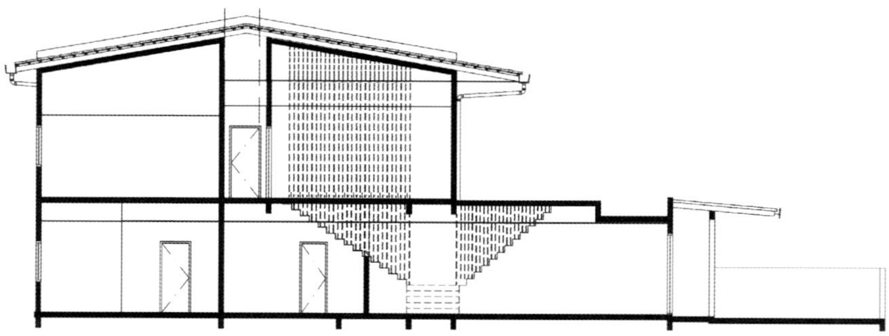

Section

On the first floor, the split staircase branches out into the terrace roof garden on one side and the private sanctum on the other on the first floor. This arrangement allows guests to access the open space without compromising the privacy of the master bedroom. The master bedroom has an en suite bathroom set within a glass enclosure, which visually amplifies the space.

The balcony was designed to celebrate the tropical weather, with a two-thirds cement-rendered floor and a strip of grass just before the frameless glass balustrade. Ten-foot-high (3-meter-high) walls flank the entire length of the terrace, with open-faced brick walls bordering the grass strip for privacy and acoustics.

To optimize indoor air exchange, there are two customized wind turbines combined with steel-framed glazed pyramids attached to built-in vents that provide the house with stack-effect ventilation. A three-degree differential is enough to spin the turbines by convection.

The new form and height of 23 Terrace are rejuvenating revisions of the 1970s single-story terrace. It is a baby step toward the greening of the neighborhood and an attempt to educate the community about the importance of green retrofitting.

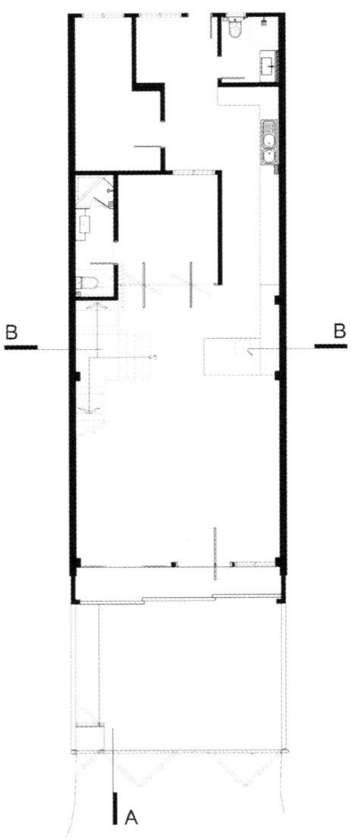

Ground-floor plan

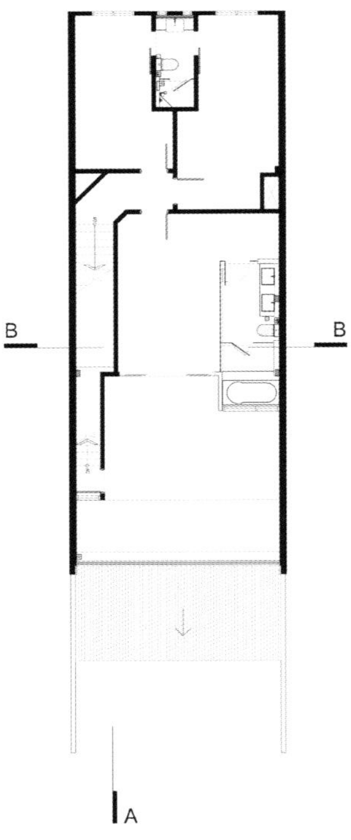

First-floor plan

KINGSWOOD

The original building on the site had to be demolished after a series of earthquakes had affected the region. The demolition revealed the original roof trusses, which were rescued and safely stored by the client, who was hoping to reuse them. The trusses became an important feature of the new building, and these were strengthened with rusted metal plates and exposed bolts.

The new building envelope needed to fit in the industrial port area and respond to the heritage constraints of the city plan. This led the design to keep the original shape of the building, reinterpreting the structure and cladding material.

The client requested an open space that celebrated the view to the port and created privacy from the surroundings. For this, the design of the big steel and cedar window facade allowed a great view to the harbor, the hill, and the stormy southerly weather.

The house was designed to expose the big steel structure and bracing elements in order to provide a sense of safety after the dramatic 2011 earthquake, and it was used to give a visual rhythm to the interior, which was otherwise a too dispersive space. The walls were built from a SIP (structural insulated panel) lightweight material to achieve greater thermal insulation.

The layout creates a feeling of openness toward the south facade, while also creating a more sheltered and intimate area in the back of the building, encouraging visitors to direct their attention toward the living area. The volumes were designed to create 'hiding' spaces. Although the whole space is actually big and open, there are many areas where one can feel protected and sheltered.

DESIGN: MC Architecture Studio
LOCATION: Christchurch, New Zealand
AREA: 4,080 square feet (379 square meters)
COMPLETION YEAR: 2015
ORIGINAL BUILDING: 1913
PHOTOGRAPHY: Mick Stephenson

TE WAIPOUNAMU THE SOUTH ISLAND

TROCADERO

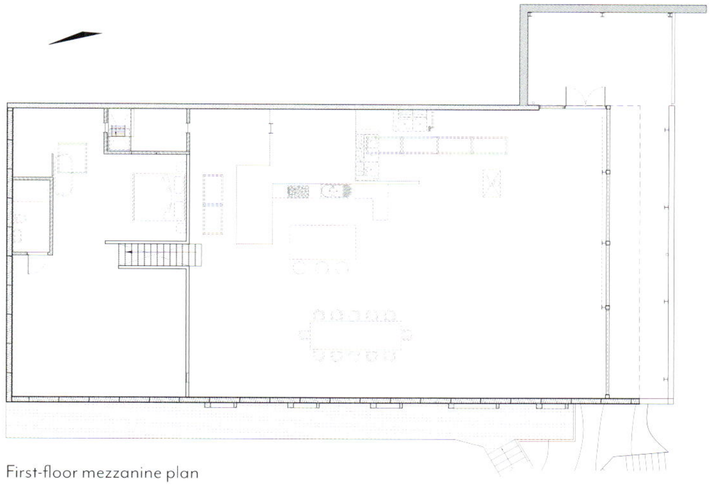

First-floor mezzanine plan

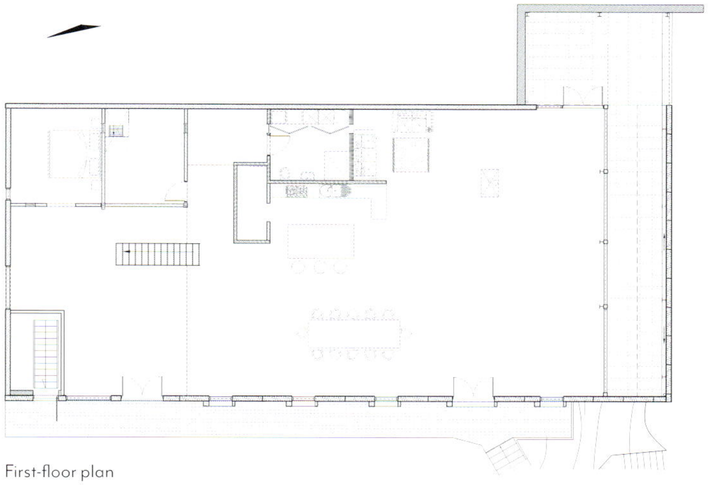

First-floor plan

BOLD HOUSE

Located in The Hague, this home was in a dilapidated state, requiring a thorough reinforcement of the foundation and load-bearing structure. This enabled some extraordinary possibilities for an otherwise commonplace apartment renovation.

The combination of ambitious design vision, and a considerable amount of trust from the client, resulted in a rigorous and uncompromising redesign, in which voids and split levels accentuate the full height of this classic Dutch row house.

According to the clients, the brick structure's potential, its glass-in-lead detailing, and classic en suite room separations were features that influenced their purchase decision. The tension between antique features and modern techniques is evident in the redesign. The classical street facade was restored to its former glory, from the ground to third floors.

A dramatic change is revealed just behind the doors of the street-facing en suite element. The rear facade was removed and clad with glass to a full height of 36 feet (11 meters). The floor levels were detached from the facade, creating a void that spans three levels and generating an optimal source of daylight.

A steel construction replaced the load-bearing wall between the corridor and the living room in the rear of the house. Four new floors with a net height of 7.9 feet (2.4 meters) protrude from this construction. These floors are open and visually connected to existing floor levels. The interplay of voids, the split-levels, and the glass facade all create a spectacular drama between interior and exterior, and between the existing and new floors.

DESIGN: Personal Architecture
LOCATION: The Hague, The Netherlands
AREA: 2,422 square feet (225 square meters)
COMPLETION YEAR: 2011
ORIGINAL BUILDING: Late 1800s
PHOTOGRAPHY: René de Wit

92
94

CHAPTER 2
THINKING MINIMALLY

RENIER CHALON

Traditionally, houses in Brussels are built following a plan of three rooms in a row. The rooms that are on the street side are prestigious spaces, while backyard rooms are dedicated to service. The central parts, which often lack direct daylight, are generally left as secondary spaces. This beautiful house, located in Ixelles, is no exception to this rule.

The project, which aimed to transform the first two levels of a house into one dwelling, took advantage of the configuration. On the street side, the rooms were perfectly restored in their original state by the conservation of their volume and the rehabilitation of their décor.

The central parts were dematerialized and transformed into a large staircase. This intervention was inspired by Belgian architect Victor Horta, who, a century ago, upset the plan of the typical Brusselian house by implanting the staircase in the center as a source of light and visual connection. The stairs were connected to large landing like a mezzanine, allowing the space to be transformed into a living area, rather than just a thoroughfare.

On the garden side, all floors and walls without heritage value were demolished. This left room for new structures that became the bedrooms. The level of the ground floor was lowered along a monumental concrete staircase, so that the kitchen and the dining room could be aligned with the garden and gain ceiling height. Lowering the level of the ground floor also allowed an integration of an additional floor by a set of split-levels and, therefore, met the needs of the client.

DESIGN: MAMOUT architectes and Atelier d'architecture AUXAU
LOCATION: Brussels, Belgium
AREA: 3,873 square feet (357 square meters)
COMPLETION YEAR: 2018
ORIGINAL BUILDING: 1910
PHOTOGRAPHY: Guy-Joël Ollivier

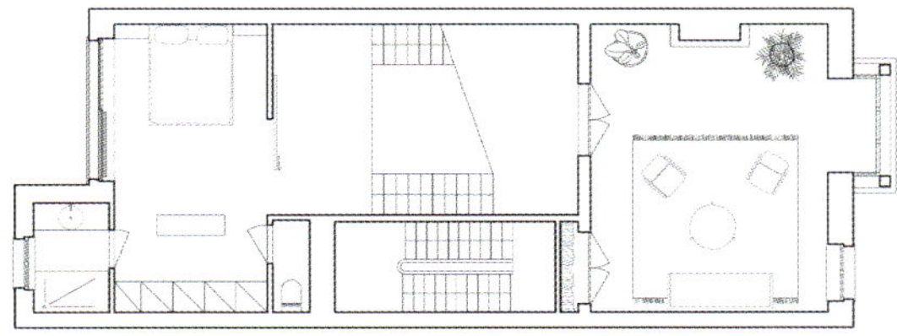

Second-floor plan

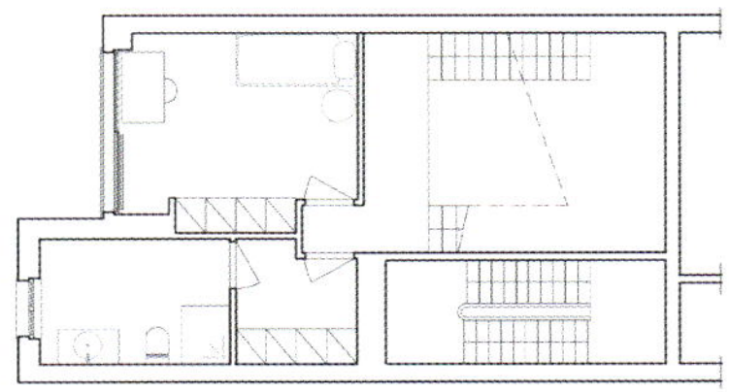

Intermediate-floor plan

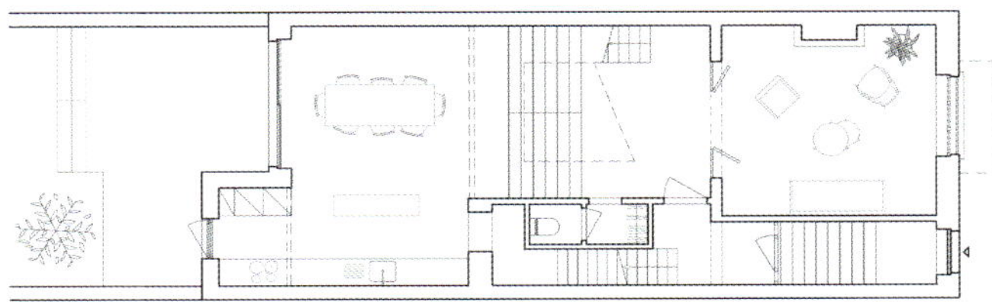

Ground-floor plan

Axonometric diagram

FOSTER ROAD RETREAT

Over the years, a series of well-intentioned accretions—ornamental dormers, an incongruous addition, and a cavernous porch—had cloaked this house, dating back to 1850, in a 'dog's dinner' of mismatched additions. The project involved demolishing these elements to make way for a sympathetic modern update of the house maintaining much of the existing exterior material, with a new diamond-patterned zinc roof that mimics the pattern the client discovered in a historic photo of the house.

The retreat's modest exterior belies the spaciousness of the main floor. At the north end, an unobtrusive, functional kitchen thickens the exterior wall with inset casework and appliances. Across the house, to the other side of the chimney and stairs, built-in shelving and storage lend the study's south exterior wall a similar depth of feel. The existing interior brick presented a significant challenge. Large portions of wall had shattered, requiring laborious reconstruction. Salvaged wood flooring carries the marks of the house's original occupants.

Anchoring the main level's composition is a remnant of the original masonry fireplace skirted by a suspended steel staircase. The staircase is a bit of a showcase, and rightfully so; it was the house's most challenging exercise. Everything about it was scrutinized and pared down to achieve required dimensions and clearances without compromising its catalytic role in the space. The stairs consist of dark solid-stock wood surfaces cradled within a welded assembly of blackened steel. Minimal handrail brackets were the only components to directly interface with the brick. Adjacent to the chimney, bent steel treads cantilever from a self-supporting steel stringer.

The staircase provides access to an intimate bedroom suite above. Dimensions here are exceedingly tight. Fully glazed dormers offer essential headroom, bathing the whitewashed original pine planks in light and framing views of trees and sky. The dormers' impact on the house's appearance is aesthetically considered. Elsewhere, the old roof's remaining nooks and crannies fit the rituals of domestic life (dressing, bathing, and laundry) like a glove.

DESIGN: Neumann Monson Architects
LOCATION: Iowa, United States
AREA: 1,538 square feet (126 square meters)
COMPLETION YEAR: 2017
ORIGINAL BUILDING: 1850
PHOTOGRAPHY: Integrated Studio

First-floor plan

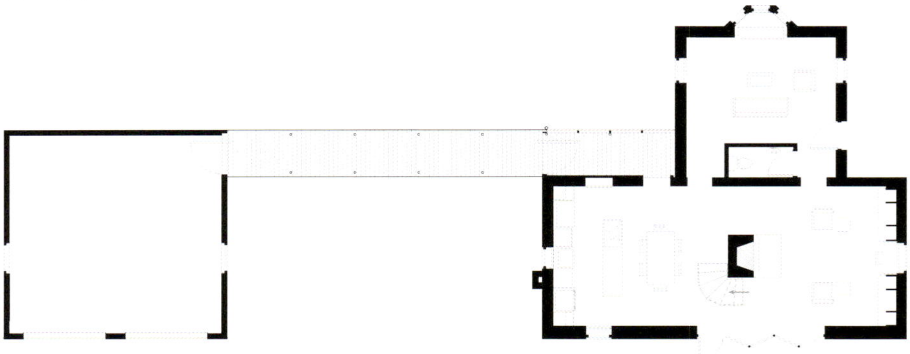

Ground-floor plan

YELLOW+TERRAZZO

This villa was set in the Brianza area, Italy, on the hills around Lecco. Here, the building landscape was clearly marked by 1970s residential construction methodologies. The restoration remodeled both distribution and composition, while maintaining the local character.

This project granted a new lease of life to the originally horizontal duplex building through a new vertical dimension, which offered both units individual panoramic views and aspects of the garden.

One the ground floor, the apartment facing northeast and, on the southwest, the second, larger apartment on multiple levels alternate and develop, embracing both the ground and first floor. In the larger unit, on two levels, space distribution began with a new staircase, which completely redefined the spaces; constructed in white coated metal, it appears as if suspended from a softly curved aperture above the kitchen area, adding character to the dining room.

All kitchen furnishings were bespoke, in dark wood, contrasting with the wide openings and light tinted walls. They completed the development of the staircase with a functional and organic design, taking the shape of a storage bench and an island with an integrated worktop.

Dark wood, in combination with the recurring color ochre, contrasts with the new glass openings and the light shades on the walls. Terrazzo flooring, used throughout the space, echoes the colors of the existing tiles on the upper floor.

On the first floor, the new bathrooms were inserted diagonally into the existing layout to define a new dynamic space, while the living room and the music room connect across the stairs in one fluid, open space. A number of round openings allowing more light in are key elements in the living area.

The master bedroom boasts two exclusive areas: a walk-in closet and private access to the new triangular balcony. All finishings are consistent with the reinterpretation approach of the original style.

DESIGN: Francesca Perani Enterprise + Bloomscape Architecture
LOCATION: Bulciago, Italy
AREA: 1,615 square feet (150 square meters)
COMPLETION YEAR: 2017
ORIGINAL BUILDING: 1970s
PHOTOGRAPHY: Francesca Perani

Significant to the project was the removal of the existing external staircase and the repositioning of the triangular balcony. In addition, new metal grates and the full reshaping of the large porch, by means of a single, articulated, colored metal element, improve privacy, and offer multifunctional outdoor spaces.

New round light apertures were inserted on all sides, including the south-facing wall, which was originally blind; they create a new balance for the composition, providing new lighting effects in all indoor spaces. The ground floor is characterized by ample mirrors connecting indoor spaces with outside areas, including a small summer solarium below ground level.

Existing openings were maintained and enriched with two-tone window frames (ochre and white) and brown roller blinds. The dark plaster was dictated by local building typologies.

Plastering, textures, window frames, and roller blinds contrasting with the external masonry were reinterpreted in a contemporary light; however, applying a sensitive restyling approach, which maintains the distinctive 1970s style.

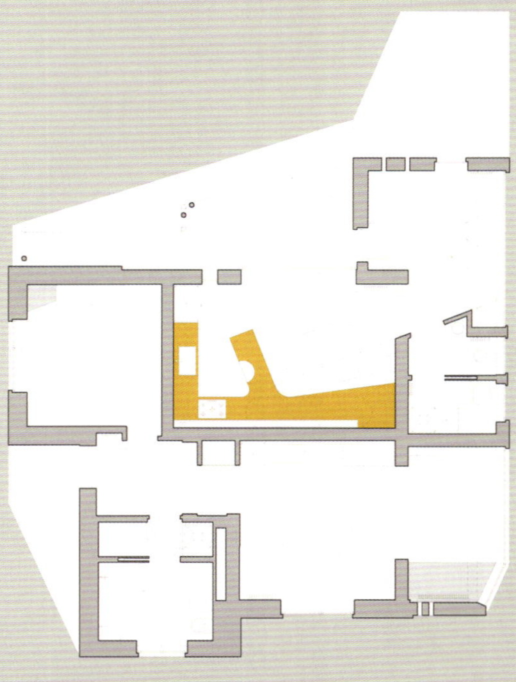

Ground-floor plan

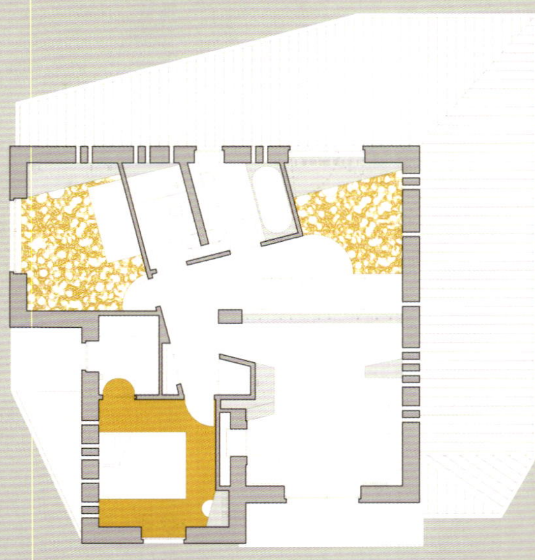

First-floor plan

VILLA CC

This house, located in Sardinia, Italy, nestles behind its walls, secretly hidden, in the small village of San Vito. For more than a century, its construction has grown from a small house to a compound including two shops, a bathroom, and other additional rooms that have all overrun the little patio.

The first step of the project was to remove all unnecessary constructions and reveal the shape and the scale of the spaces. The corridors were removed and all the new circulation was organized around two central spaces (one on the first floor and one on the entrance floor).

New openings through the thick walls (built with river stones) connect and filter these central spaces to the more intimate and quiet rooms: the bedrooms and the living room.

On the ground floor the absence of doors reveals unexpected views from the inner rooms to the patio through the dining room and the kitchen. Continuity and permeability of the spaces cohabitate with intimacy and quietness. A guest room with an en suite bathroom is also located on the corner of the entrance floor.

The more private and quiet first floor accommodates four bedrooms and two bathrooms. A shared living room offers a privileged view of the patio.

DESIGN: Matteo Foresti Architecture Studio AB
LOCATION: Sardinia, Italy
AREA: 2,798 square feet (260 square meters)
COMPLETION YEAR: 2017
ORIGINAL BUILDING: Early 1900s
PHOTOGRAPHY: Atelier XYZ

Section

The central rooms work also as a filter for the intense light coming from the patio so that just a soft reflected light can fill the bedrooms and the living room. The rooms are dominated by clean lines and by the use of white plaster that finishes interiors and the exteriors.

A solid gray porphyry covers the exterior surfaces, a raw texture that ends as soon as you approach the interior of the house. Here white Carrara marble tiles with a matt finish create a soft and delicate surface to walk on barefoot. On the first floor all the rooms share a white-washed oak wood floor, while the bathrooms continue the use of Carrara marble.

In the patio, by preserving a thick wall from one of the former shops and removing the roof, a new space was created: a 'secret garden,' a room open to the sky.

Between the inside and the outside, the white walls have become the silent background for some family memories under the intense sunlight of Sardinia.

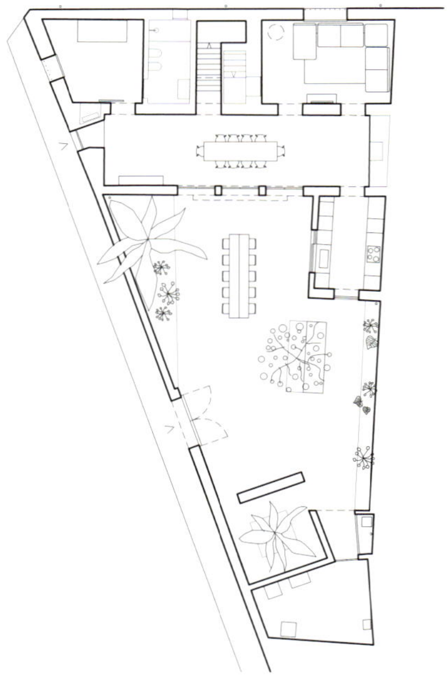

Floor plan

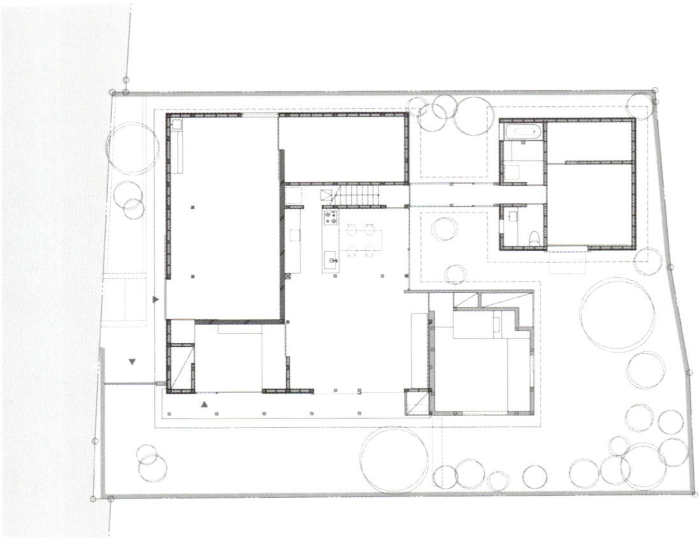

Ground-floor plan

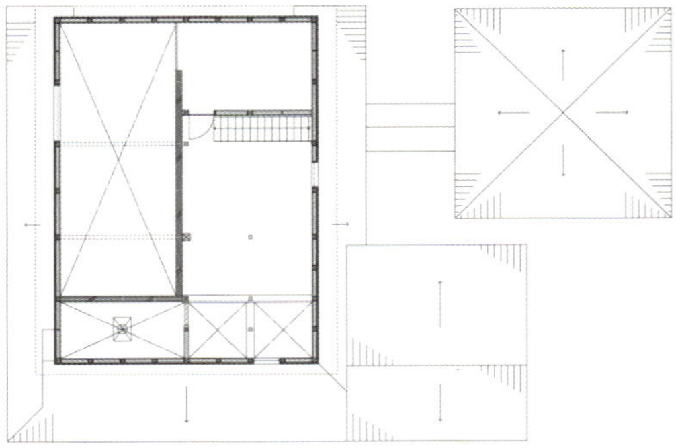

First-floor plan

RESIDENCE MARIBOU

DESIGN: Alain Carle Architecte
LOCATION: Saint-Sauveur, Canada
AREA: 2,422 square feet (225 square meters)
COMPLETION YEAR: 2016
ORIGINAL BUILDING: 1960s
PHOTOGRAPHY: Raphael Thibodeau

This 1960s house featured the traits of that period's Scandinavian architecture, and followed the importance of functionality and materiality, which would be the keys to design. This 'organic' architecture was brought to the forefront in this transformation.

Although this house had several insulation and structural problems, its great singularity motivated the owners to invest in its renovation, instead of in a total demolition. The objective thus was to conserve its original character, while modernizing several of its aspects to improve the program's functionality.

Apart from the restoration of the envelope and several interior elements, the main challenge was to review access in order to reduce the number of steps to climb from the parking. The main entrance, previously located on the second floor, was relocated to the first floor, forcing a complete reorganization of traffic and the program. A new arch signals this intervention and emphasizes the new route.

Previously topped with a flat roof, the project added a pitched roof that was thought to correspond better to its original Scandinavian essence. Given the local bylaws required a pitched roof, the idea was to negotiate the roof profile to return to a more coherent volumetric architecture.

The projecting side walls delimiting the house were also a key component of the initial construction. Unfortunately, these walls had been relegated to the background by the roof that covered them. In this same logic of respecting the original character, these walls were widened and highlighted by the contrast of different materials. For the interior, the strong elements represented by the big stone wall and the singular railing were conserved in their entirety and restored to context in a more contemporary composition.

The new volumetry, freeing more space in the master bedroom, allows the addition of new fenestration opening on the landscape. On the main floor, new openings were made to finally give a view of the rocky landscape from the kitchen. The residence, which previously had a back room exclusively orientated to the distant view, now offers a multitude of framings of different landscape scales.

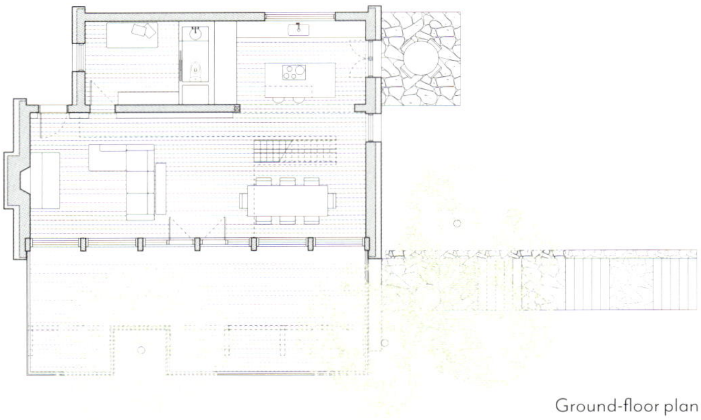

Ground-floor plan

Elevation

CASA VI

DESIGN: Alfredo Vanotti Architetto, EV+A lab Atelier d'Architettura & Interior Design
LOCATION: Piateda, Italy
AREA: 807 square feet (75 square meters)
COMPLETION YEAR: 2015
ORIGINAL BUILDING: 1970s
PHOTOGRAPHY: Marcello Mariana

This project is located in the Orobic Alps at 3,280 feet (1,000 meters) above sea level. The client wished to transform an existing ruin, built originally from concrete bricks, into a residence that had ample sunlight and lighting in the living room and, at the same time, a view toward the bottom of the valley.

After a careful analysis of the context—of the possibilities in terms of exposure, the study of the sunlight, the study of technologies, and the values of mountain architecture—the designers sought to create a modern aesthetic but chose to employ the construction techniques and materials used in the past. The architects believe that mountain architecture is an emblematic example of sustainable architecture, and also used natural materials and, for obvious reasons, found in situ. From a formal point of view, the residence makes reference to the rural local houses, although the cottage has the only sloping roof and it's completely faced by stone and has no eaves.

The architects concentrated on the insulation and lighting, as the Orobic Alps are poorly exposed to natural sunlight. Opting for the coverage to a single aquifer allowed the architects to raise the exposed wall to the north, inserting four openings of equal size: one room on the first floor and two on the ground floor with a wonderful view of the mountains. This also gave a double height to the kitchenette and dining area, with a skylight providing natural illumination. As a result, a bright and naturally lit house was achieved.

The house was constructed with reinforced concrete and concrete bricks, with suitable thermal insulation, in order to obtain a good level of household comfort. The exterior was veneered in local stone. Inside larch wood beams are painted white, to create a sense of space, while the doors and windows are made of brushed lamellar larch, bestowing a warmth. The architects aimed to achieve the greatest possible outcome using materials at hand, such as reinforced concrete, natural larch, iron, and wood.

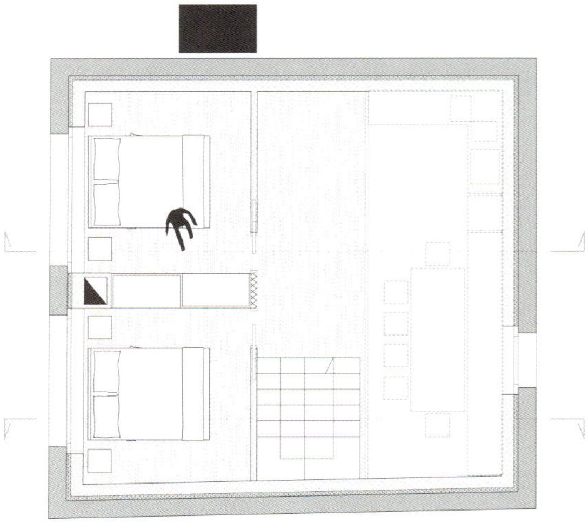

First-floor plan

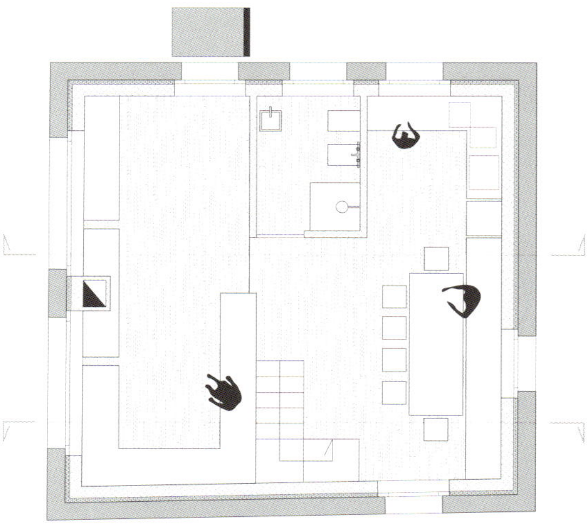

Ground-floor plan

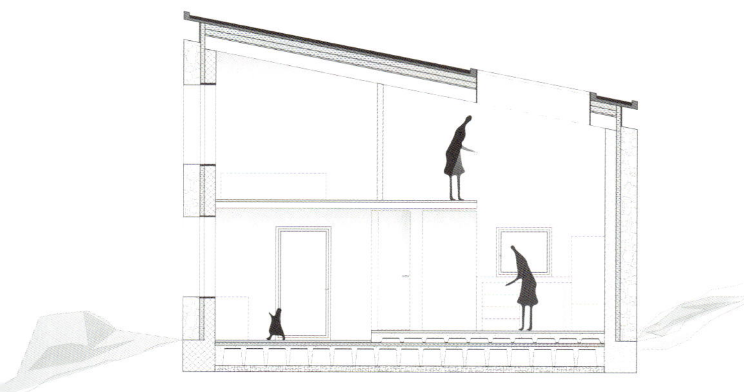

Section

ICHIJOJI HOUSE

The designers applied traditional finishes and techniques to the design and renovation of this postwar terraced house. The client, a Danish–Australian furniture maker, wished to modernize the home without abandoning the character that makes traditional Japanese houses unique. From this respect, a design approach was adopted whereby modern attitudes to living would be balanced and contrasted with tradition.

Originally constructed in 1961 as one in a block of four homes, this typical exemplar of the postwar Japanese row house typology had been left largely unaltered and allowed to dilapidate for more than half a century. The project brief called for extensive renovation of the existing home and a small extension at the rear to accommodate new indoor plumbing and increased flexibility of use.

Unlike many similar renovations in Japan, which erase historical building stock through the unremarkable application of low durability prefabricated systems, an unconventional application of traditional techniques and materials allowed for the retention and enhancement of much of the home's traditional character. From the stained wallpaper and lacquered floorboards to the timber joinery, every element was handfinished using traditional techniques.

DESIGN: atelier Luke
LOCATION: Kyoto, Japan
AREA: 538 square feet (50 square meters)
COMPLETION YEAR: 2015
ORIGINAL BUILDING: 1961
PHOTOGRAPHY: Eiji Kitada + atelier Luke

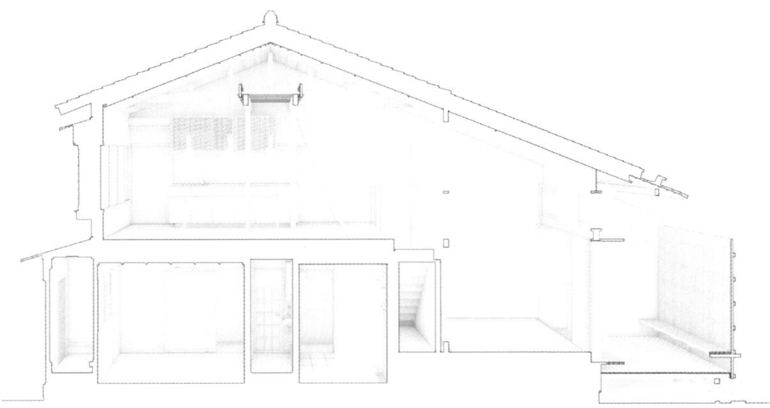

Section

Existing structural timber elements were also alternately concealed and revealed to experiment with and occasionally subvert traditional Japanese approaches to building character. In some cases, such as with the large cambered roof beams, previously hidden elements were celebrated as striking sculptural forms within the home.

Programmatically, the house was inverted from its original design; with living spaces placed on the upper floor and private areas on the ground. A sensitively flexible and multileveled living, dining, and kitchen space transformed the spatial and experiential qualities of the interior. New prospects to the outdoors and an increased sense of spaciousness were provided by a screened courtyard, which flows from the living space through layers of sliding timber doors and paper screens.

The old ground floor kitchen was converted into a traditional Japanese bedroom, with tatami mats, shoji screens, and handmade wallpaper. A new bathroom and toilet on the ground floor replaced outbuildings that were demolished to allow for an extension of the house. In these private and contained spaces, lacquered wallpapers brought a vibrancy of color in contrast the warm neutrality of the living areas.

A series of bespoke furniture pieces were also created. Japanese oak kitchen cabinetry was combined with a unique copper worktop and services ducting, resulting in a sensitively utilitarian aesthetic that complements the raw materiality of the home. A fixed oak dining table was supported from the building structure, allowing it to almost float in space. Finally, a timber ladder provides both access to a small loft as well as an invitation to touch and grasp these specially crafted elements.

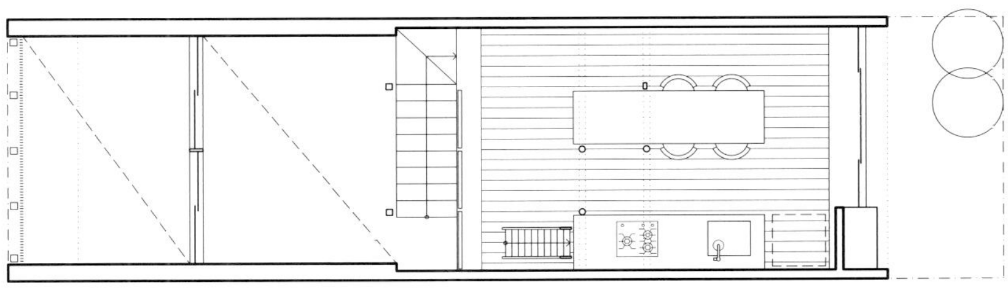

First-floor plan

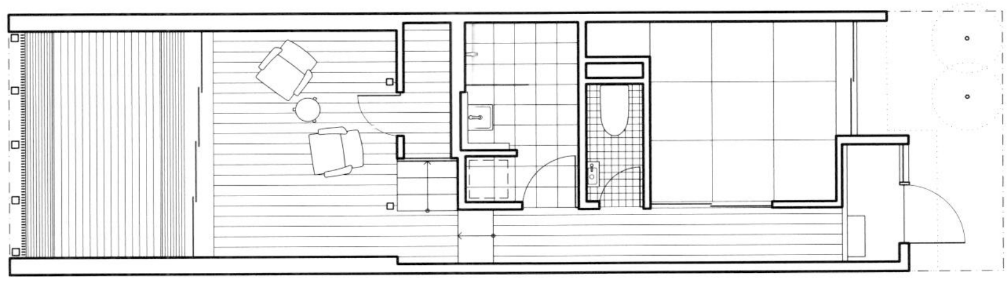

Ground-floor plan

LAKE FOREST PARK HOUSE

Located on a secluded, wooded site north of Seattle, a 1950s Northwest contemporary house was completely renovated while retaining the spirit of the original residence. With extensive new windows and glazed roof monitors, the renovated house appears to be a glass pavilion in the forest.

The floor plan was reorganized to create a spacious, light-filled master bedroom and master bath, with each space surrounded by glass and views to the forest. The main living and dining spaces were slightly enlarged, and a new roof monitor with high windows was added to bring soft natural light to the entire space. The new, enlarged kitchen was fitted with counters in quartz and cast-glass, with continuous windows extending directly to the counter level.

The existing hemlock ceiling with exposed fir beams in roughly half the house were retained, and new fir ceilings were added to the remainder of the house. The existing terrazzo flooring was refinished, with new areas of terrazzo added in a complementary color.

Consistent with the original simplicity and clarity of the house, a palette of new materials was added to create powerful juxtapositions of texture and color, allowing each material to benefit from adjacent contrasting surfaces. The casework consists primarily of cherry panels: some panels are smooth while others were milled with a CNC (computer numeric controlled) router to make a texture evocative of 'woven wood.' An accent wall adjacent to the dining and kitchen areas was clad entirely in weathered steel panels. Suspended casework on the steel wall utilizes either resin panels with natural grasses or textured cherry wood, both materials set against the variegated umber colors of the steel.

DESIGN: FINNE Architects
LOCATION: Seattle, United States
AREA: 3,100 square feet (288 square meters)
COMPLETION YEAR: 2012
ORIGINAL BUILDING: 1950s
PHOTOGRAPHY: Benjamin Benschneider Photography

Custom fabrications included the cast-glass kitchen counter, steel wall panels, suspended steel mirror frames, laser-cut steel shade valences, custom steel lighting bars, hand-blown glass light fixtures (TROMS pendants), and a number of custom furniture pieces. The glass wall between the master bedroom and master bathroom was transformed with the use of a hand-drawn pattern in etched glass, with the pattern being denser at the bottom (for a sense of privacy) and increasingly transparent at the top.

Sustainable design practices were integral to the project from the start. Radiant heating under the terrazzo flooring created an even heat source with maximum energy efficiency. High clerestory windows bring natural light deep into the house and motorized operators allow for venting during summer months. Many green materials (such as resin panels, quartz counters, linoleum, low VOC paint, and sustainable wood products) were used in the project. But above all, it is the fact of renovation itself that is inherently sustainable and captures all the embodied energy of the original 1950s house, which was given a fresh life. The intense craftsmanship and detailing of the renovation speaks also to a very important sustainable principle: build it well and it will last for many, many years.

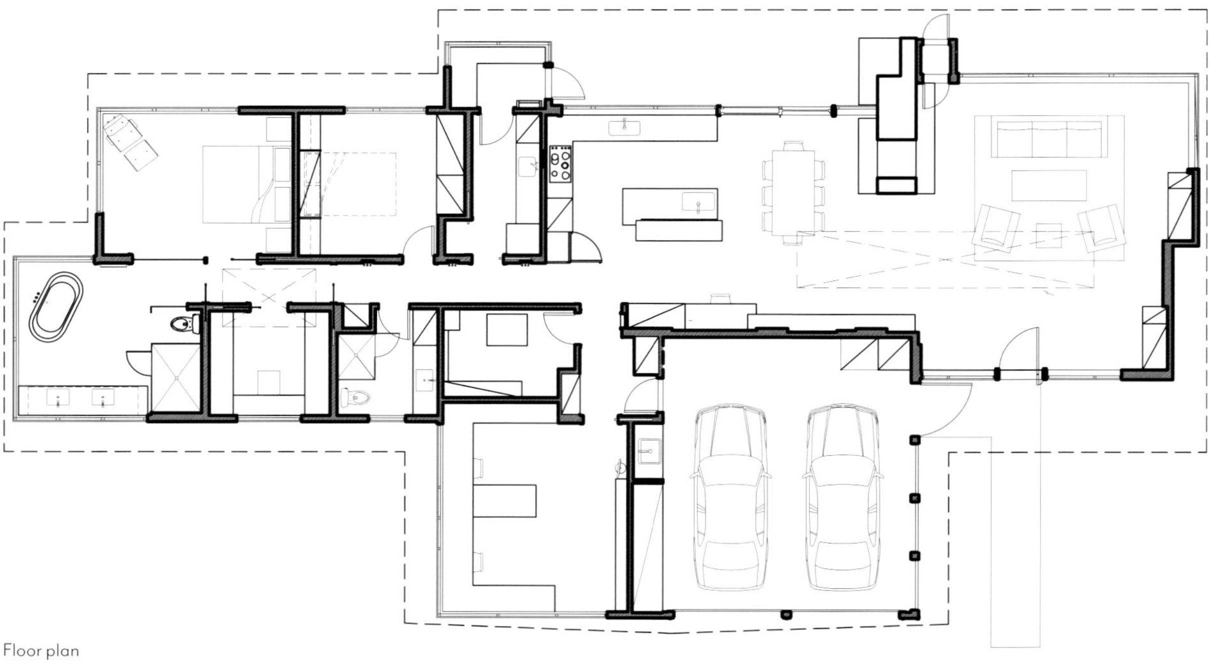

Floor plan

CHAPTER 3

A GROWING FAMILY

A WHITE HOUSE

This project involved the renovation of a three-story white residence located on an old lane in Shanghai and surrounded by many similar buildings in a naturally formed block.

The original architecture was completed in 1947 and had entrances on both sides. Due to the complicated compartments and deep depth, the overall indoor lighting was very poor.

The designer began by reinforcing the whole building and unified the height of the structure. The staircase on the northern side was torn down. A skylight and staircase were designed to be the center of the building, reshaping the logic and form of the three-story building. The steel stairs bring in light through punched holes and they spread upward around the natural light patio on the first floor, extending the whole house vertically around the light.

A semi-opened area was designed on the first floor, which blurs the boundary between indoor and outdoor. After reconstruction, the original isolated courtyard was given a new connection with the tri-level space. The semi-outdoor area added warmth to living room. Sunshine, plants, and the blurry boundary between interior and exterior allow the inhabitants to switch freely between the usage of the spaces. A place was reserved in the courtyard to plant a tree in spring, which could accompany the kids as they grew up, making time another element of the design.

On the first floor, the sun-filled living and dining room and the kitchen were designed as a united space, where the family could spend most of their time together. The designer hoped to create a multifunctional space, rather than just an area defined by function. A modular furniture wall called 'life board' was created that could be decorated or assembled with accessories in diverse ways, along with life-changing events. As such, the designer hoped the future form of the design could be gradually shaped by the daily life of the inhabitants.

DESIGN: RIGI DESIGN
LOCATION: Shanghai, China
AREA: 2,583 square feet (240 square meters)
COMPLETION YEAR: 2017
ORIGINAL BUILDING: 1947
PHOTOGRAPHY: TIAN Fangfang

On the second floor, the door and the storage space were hidden behind the wall, which creates a feeling of additional space. Particular attention was given to the design of the child's room, with the child's bed, desk, and storage space connected through the design.

Following natural daylight, going up along the steel staircase, the design offers modified skylights, vertical lighting windows, and a pure outdoor space. The whole building starts from light and vertical space. For the main bedroom, the designer kept the slope structure of the original building, unified the cloakroom and the toilet into a box, reserving the original architectural form to the largest extent and creating a new connection in the original space, which is not big.

"We wanted to design something carrying beauty and happiness," said the designers. "There is not so much joy in life, and our life is filled with small happiness. What we love is not to possess good things or luxurious furniture, but a self-made life on our own. Having seen so many houses, the only concept we believe is that a person cannot be stuck with a settled life, whether in the house value or style."

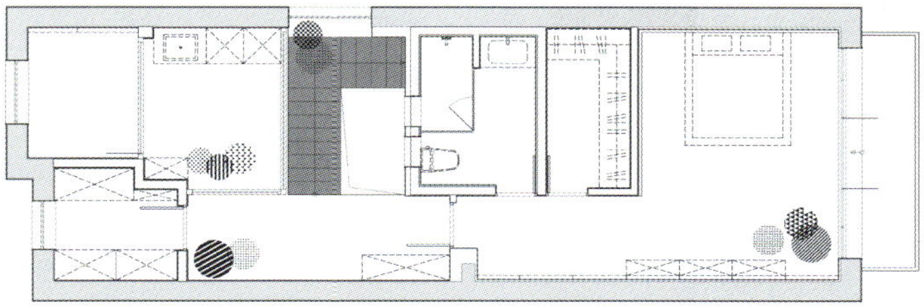

Second-floor plan

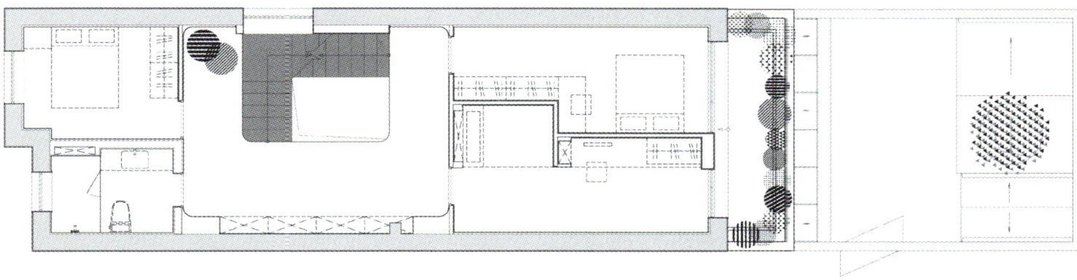

First-floor plan

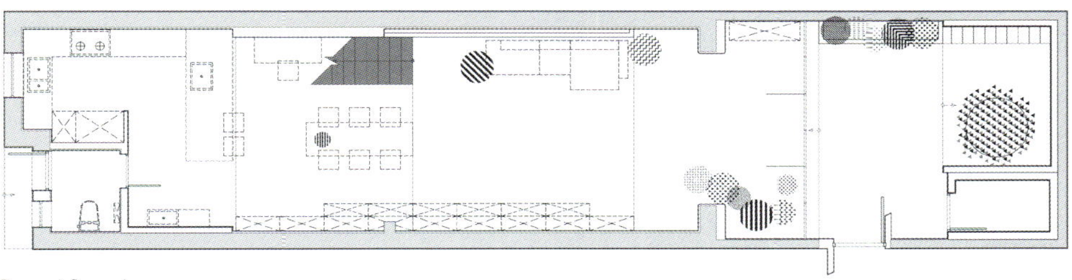

Ground-floor plan

BEIJING

Le sac
en papier

ATELIER 142

Located in a small cobbled street typical of Paris, an old garage was transformed into a painter's studio in the 1970s by the painter, Pierre Lemaire. Almost 50 years later, Pierre's granddaughter sought to transform her grandfather's studio into a living space, and contacted Willy Durieu, founder of Atelier WILDA.

The project consisted of the transformation of the little workspace into a minimalist loft in the heart of Paris. However, urban regulations in this part of the city are very strict and prohibited any modification of the existing volume. All work, therefore, had to be done internally, optimizing every inch of space.

The entire existing interior design and the slab were demolished, preserving only the load-bearing walls and the roof and revealing a large open volume of space, ripe for transformation. The ceilings were removed, and openings created throughout the house thus retaining the feeling and perception of space. The light floods this beautiful space through the large glass facade and generous roof windows.

A muted color spectrum was used in order to amplify the sense of space, while white walls highlight the wooden elements (beech), softening the light and creating a warm atmosphere. Custom furniture has been designed to the smallest detail in order to optimize all possible storage spaces while adapting perfectly to the petite size of the loft. The architect proposed an internal cabin-like structure perched at the top of the volume with a bird's-eye view of the living room, an ingenious idea which created an extra chamber containing a workspace with storage, a foldaway desk, and a large bed for two people.

DESIGN: Atelier WILDA
LOCATION: Paris, France
AREA: 538 square feet (50 square meters)
COMPLETION YEAR: 2017
ORIGINAL BUILDING: 1970s
PHOTOGRAPHY: David Foessel

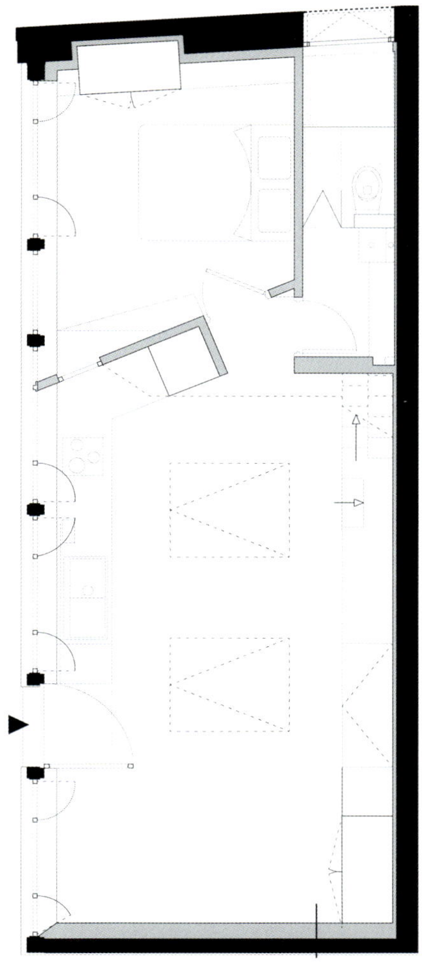

Ground-floor plan

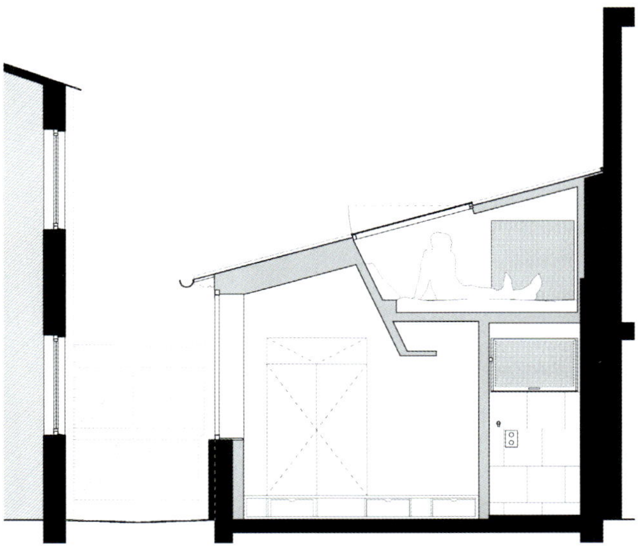

Section

GLOUTON
Le Croqueur de Livres

THE BOUNDARYLESS HOUSE

Dating back to 1919, this three-story house, located in Guangzhou's old central business district, was a classic, narrow townhouse. Due to the inappropriate setting of the windows, neither natural ventilation nor light could easily enter the house, causing a serious problem in terms of darkness and humidity. Along with the structural problems due to the disrepair of the house, these issues had compounded to become troubling for the daily livelihood of the family.

Decades ago, the house had been divided into many individual spaces, to accommodate the couple with their five children. No longer housing a large family, those individual spaces were not only empty, but had also become boundaries within the home. The designer sought to create more space for family members' interactions and togetherness through his design. His focus was on improving family relationships by better utilizing the space.

The house originally consisted of living zones separated by a solid wall. Therefore, the designer decided to connect these two sections by removing the load-bearing wall and rebuilding the steel structure in order to change the entire floor plan. The second step was to design a core tube, which combined the main movement line of the family (stairs and elevator), and to rearrange the scattered spaces. resulting in a better interconnect with each room in the house.

After removing all of the nonfunctional boundaries and rearranging the whole floor plan, residents were able to walk more freely and have interactions with each other in the house. Furthermore, by utilizing the front and backyard, skylight and open space, more sunlight could shine into the house, solving any ventilation and lighting issues.

Originally, the first floor was separated by two rooms and had no open space. The designer changed the original structure and created a new open space, and with the reconfiguration of furniture, the first floor gained more function. The kitchen bench was extended to the outdoor garden. When sunny, the family can enjoy coffee, looking at the plants, without the need to walk outside.

DESIGN: Inspiration Group
LOCATION: Guangzhou, China
AREA: 4,036 square feet (375 square meters)
COMPLETION YEAR: 2017
ORIGINAL BUILDING: 1919
PHOTOGRAPHY: Zaohui Huang

Between the second and the third floors, the designer created a room with split-level floors specifically for leisure and cultural activities to commemorate the father, as well as the precious memory and heritage he left for the family. All bedrooms were situated on the second and third floor. After ensuring everyone's privacy, the designer created multiple sighting intersects using cavities, opposite windows, and special door settings. This worked to reduce the feeling of separation in the house.

As the family continues to grow, there was a need to consider adding more space for family members. An additional space was located on the third floor with a separate bathroom and a guest bedroom. The room doors can be opened in both directions in order to combine them as one.

Every space in the house was linked with a large cavity or skylight. In addition to allowing more natural light in the house—as long as the curtain is opened—the design also allows family member to see other rooms in the house, which creates more social interactions.

A family workshop and rooftop garden were positioned on the top floor, and additional areas for plants were incorporated into the rooftop garden. The old mottled walls and green pots together provide an interesting view. In this busy city, the family has its own little green world.

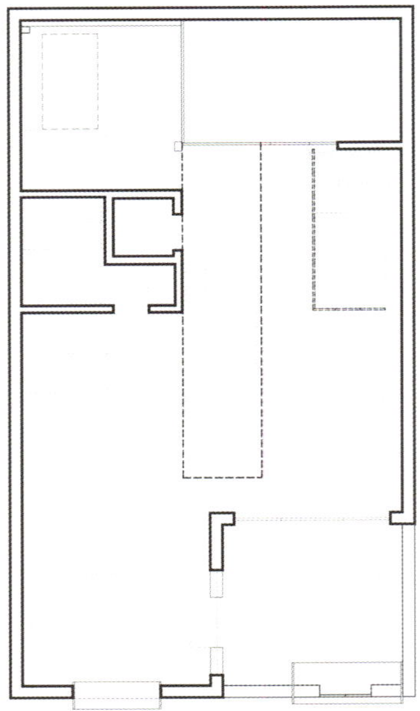

Ground-floor plan

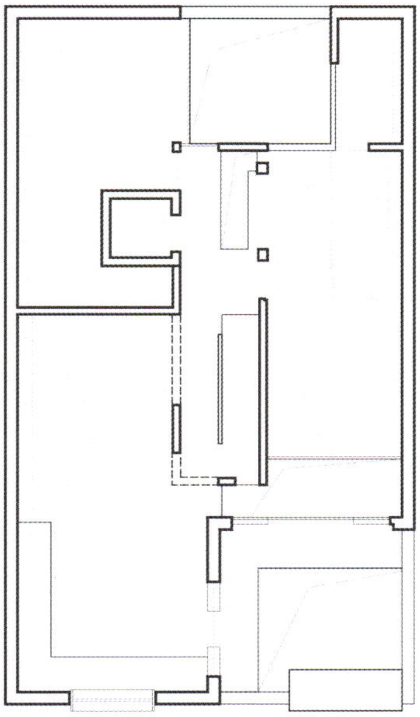

First-floor plan

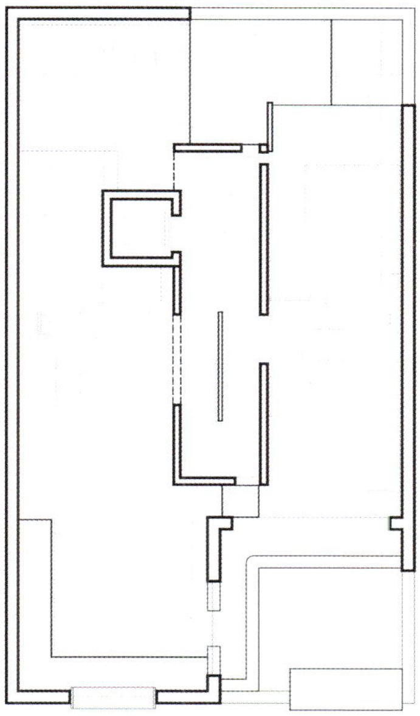

Second-floor plan

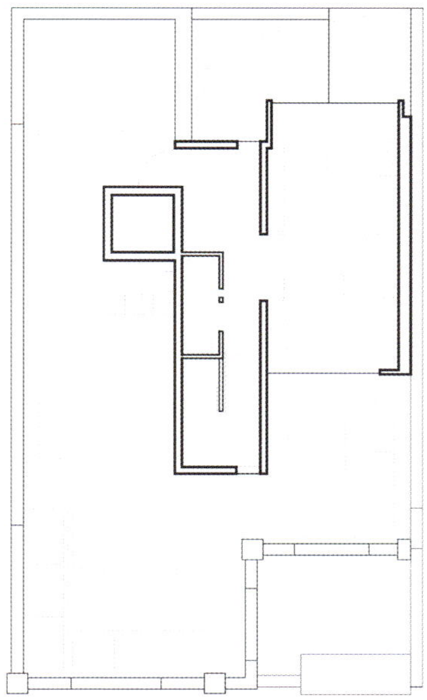

Third-floor plan

宏巨资本

CLIFTON HILL HOUSE 2

The owners requested an extension to the existing house that was generous, open, simple, and unencumbered by notions of style or luxury. The renovation was a virtual rebuilding of the salvageable front of the existing semidetached Victorian dwelling, with a dramatically different, almost separate, rear addition, which houses the main living spaces of the residence.

The existing house was stripped back to its original features, which had been obscured by 100 years of occupation. The original floorboards were replaced, and timber and plaster features revived, to create simple, uncluttered spaces, all in white, except for the black-tiled bathroom.

The proportions of the Victorian-era rooms were prefect for three bedrooms and a study room, so the addition concentrated on living spaces, which were connected to the garden on three sides.

The addition is separated from the existing house by a glazed walkway, allowing a respectful distance between old and new, as well as creating intimate courtyard-garden spaces for the bathroom and study. The living spaces and parents' level are housed in the rear pavilion, which provides the open-plan layout desired by the owners, suited to informal living with two small children.

The materials are simple exposed brickwork and concrete with black-framed glazing. This gives an uncluttered feel, but still has the warmth provided by the brickwork and garden views. The semicircular cutout garden serves to subtly divide the dining, kitchen, and lounge areas and provide a focal point for all these spaces. The inward orientation suits the inner suburban context, and once the garden is fully established, the house will be a private oasis, seemingly far removed from its close neighbors.

The owners now have ample room for a growing family and space for working from home, which is crucial when juggling the needs of small children. The openness of the space and connection to the garden allows for easy interaction and supervision of children. The simple robust finishes inside and out make for a low-maintenance environment—relaxed and comfortable.

DESIGN: ITN Architects
LOCATION: Melbourne, Australia
AREA: 3,013 square feet (280 square meters)
COMPLETION YEAR: 2017
ORIGINAL BUILDING: 1917
PHOTOGRAPHY: Aidan Halloran

BREAD

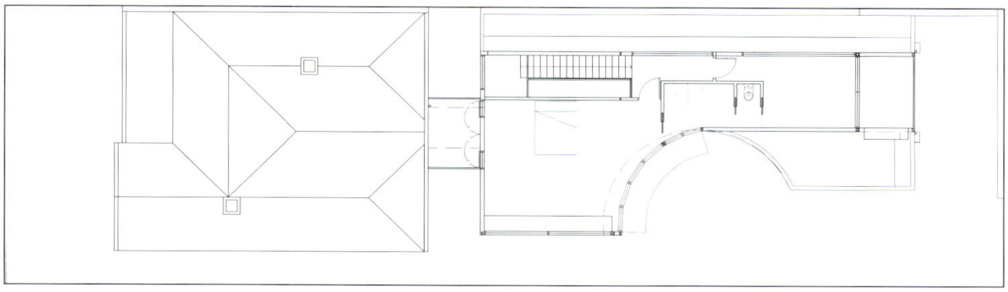

First-floor plan

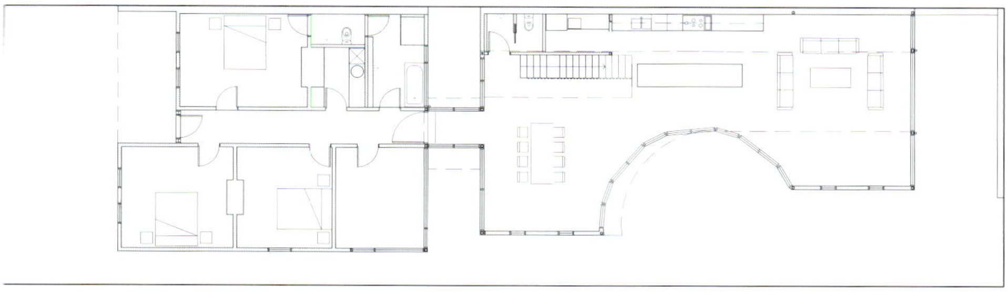

Ground-floor plan

GC HOUSE

The project involved a complete renovation of a Victorian terraced house in West London, and included a kitchen extension, loft, and basement conversion. Dating back to the 1870s as a Victorian mid-terraced house in Fulham, London, with the garden facing south and front elevation facing north, the house had its original split levels with a side kitchen extension and a loft conversion in place, but it was very dated. The original timber structure was not in very good condition in several parts of the house, so the client decided to refurbish the complete house as well as increased the size extending in the basement in just one level.

Natural light was at the heart of this project. Born out of the need to expand the Victorian property for a growing family, the core ambition was to create a flexible living space that reflected a new approach to contemporary design, characterized by light and simplicity.

Minimal sightlines and subtle textures generate a sense of relaxation and harmony, while glass and Douglas fir run throughout the home to create a series of interconnected spaces that inspire social and flexible living. A glass staircase links all floors, allowing light to flow effortlessly through the property, with views up through the home to create a sense of space and continuity.

The aim to perceive the full width of the property was important, too, especially in the reception room and in the loft. For that reason, the architect designed a suspended fireplace and the entrance cupboard to make possible the view of the two-party walls, so the property looks as wide as possible. Also, in the loft, he used smart glass in the shower to see the party wall from the head of the bed, so it looks more spacious.

The detailing around the loft was to create a very bright and light environment. All profiles used are minimal or hidden in order to achieve the lightness. Therefore, the lightness makes you feel more energetic and free independent of the season of the year.

DESIGN: Iñaki Leite architect
LOCATION: London, United Kingdom
AREA: 3,189 square feet (296 square meters)
COMPLETION YEAR: 2016
ORIGINAL BUILDING: 1870s
PHOTOGRAPHY: Adrián Vázquez

Another important element of the project was the link between the entertainment, reception room, and kitchen areas. The space flows, bringing light from the double aspect windows and skylight, but, most importantly, it is linked so that you can have a conversation when you are in different levels. Socially the house improved a lot thanks to the position of the wide staircase in the center of the house.

All furniture and lighting of the house were designed specifically for this project by the lead designer: bar, basins, cupboards, doors, kitchen cabinets, and island, railings, and so forth. The architect paid very close attention of the lighting design so as not to create dramatic shadows. The lighting design aims for a very smooth and gentle light as well as creating a relaxing space with clean lines.

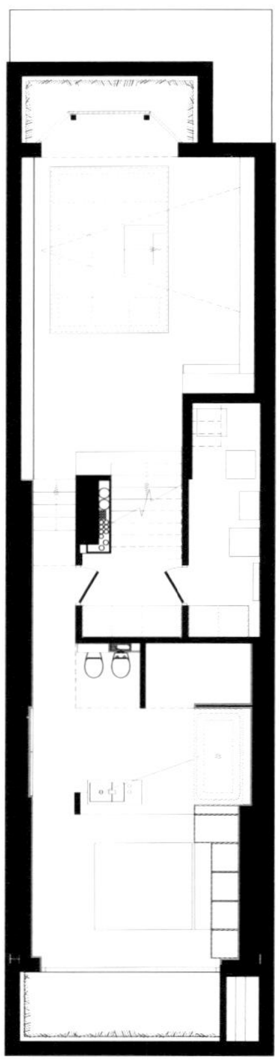

Basement floor plan

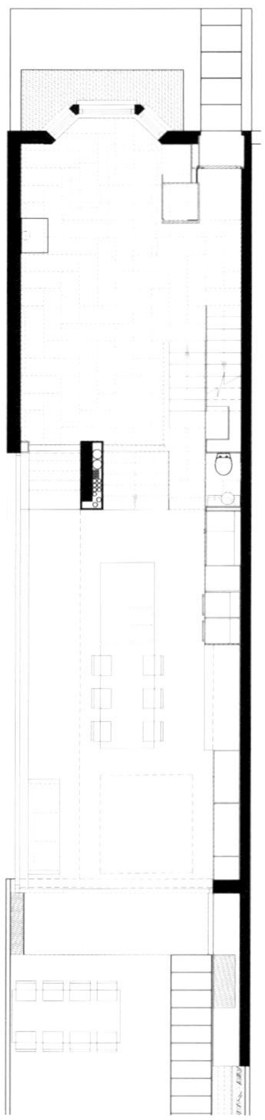

Ground-floor plan

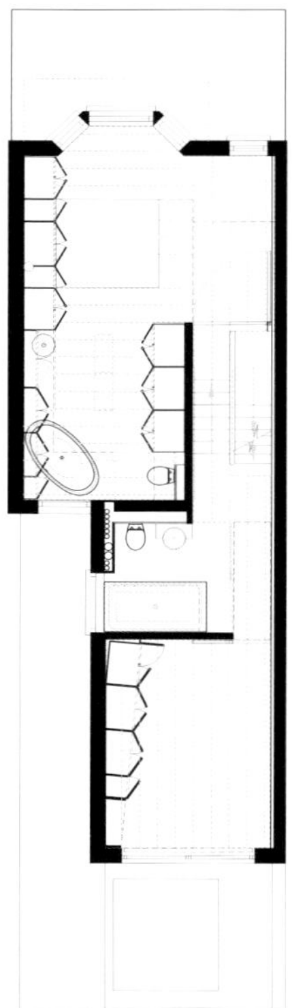

First-floor plan

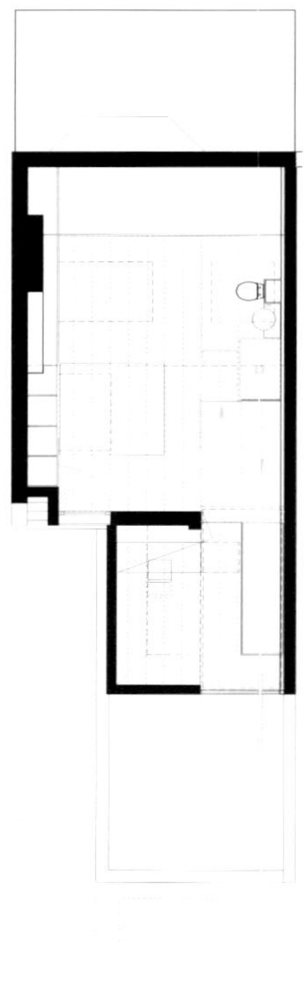

Loft plan

h&f
P
Mon - Sat
9am - 5pm
Permit holders X
or
Pay at machine
Display ticket
MATCH DAY
RESTRICTIONS
9am - 9.30pm
including
Sunday and
bank holidays
Max stay 1 hour
for pay and display

WATERLINE HOUSE

The task for this project was to organize a comfortable space for the life of a creative family with two children. Work was to be done with two apartments, which occupied the second floor of a two-story house from the 1930s. It was important to connect a contemporary renovated house with the existing architectural context of the old city.

During the renovation of the shape of the house, the total area and the configuration of the openings remained almost unchanged. Even the requirement of replacing old windows with panoramic ones with a view of the river did not outweigh the energy-saving factors and the desire to preserve the authenticity of the building. For the same reason, galvanized iron was chosen for the rooftop, as it is the most common roofing material in this part of the city. The dense gray color of the facade made it possible for the construction to drown into the shadow of the environment.

The entrance group and the connection between two houses emphasized the delicacy of the designing approach. The main entrance was given special attention, as it was a public space and common space. Light, almost airy, the staircase connects to the old beam and uncovered brickwork of the early twentieth century.

DESIGN: Ryntovt Design
LOCATION: Kharkiv, Ukraine
AREA: 2,497 square feet (232 square meters)
COMPLETION YEAR: 2017
ORIGINAL BUILDING: 1930s
PHOTOGRAPHY: Andrey Avdeenko

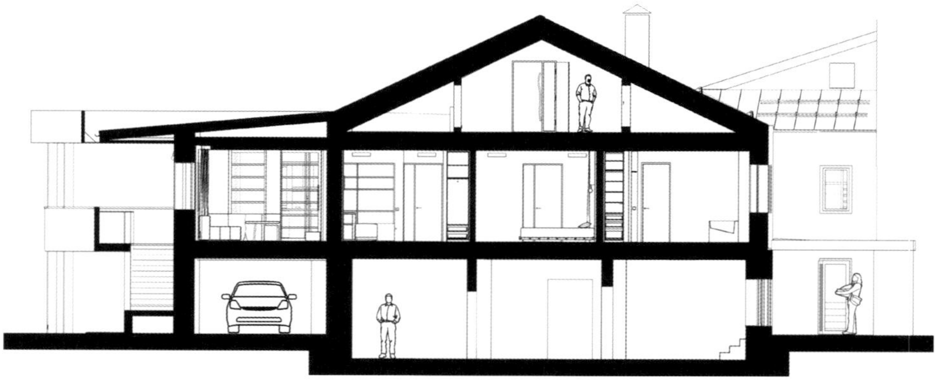

South-north section

The interior navigation was built on horizontal and vertical links: connecting volumes and visual beacons already at the entrance reveal the main axis of space. The pylons made from an ash-tree array with a forest print on them and a load-bearing wall, which goes though the bedroom of the owners of the house, a bathroom, a wardrobe, and a central hall, set up the main accents in the house.

The long hall, which connects all the spaces, reveals the entrance to the attic floor. To avoid the feeling of being in a tunnel, one of the rooms is screened by a system of partitions made of solid wood, glass, and dry grass with a swinging door block in it.

The same partition system performs the function of zoning between the living/dining room and the kitchen, but with a sliding door. The zoning of the whole space contributes to the natural insulation of all spaces. An example is the long hall: with no openings in it and no direct natural sunlight it didn't need extra heating in winter or cooling in summer. However, due to the partitions and translucency of the space, enough daylight has been achieved.

In total, the project involved four rooms: a master bedroom with en suite and wardrobe, two children's rooms, one of which has its own bathroom and a wardrobe, plus a guest room that could also work as an office.

A monochromatic palette of the interior emphasizes the democracy of space and gives it a meditative character. Paper-like snow-white curtains in the living room, a combination of dry grass, glass, and solid ash wood in the screening of the office and kitchen spaces creates an atmosphere of asceticism of Scandinavian and Japanese interiors.

The internal white and gray surfaces were 'painted' with shades created from screened partitions and light apertures in massive door blocks. These apertures have decorative doors on wooden hinges and they are also an important navigation part of the project and they give visual focus in the volume.

The interior of Waterline House has been filled with local products and ornaments, including carpets made from Carpathian wool by Ukrainian craftsmen employing traditional techniques. All furniture has been designed and produced by Ryntovt Design, which emphasizes the importance of a delicate individual approach to any project.

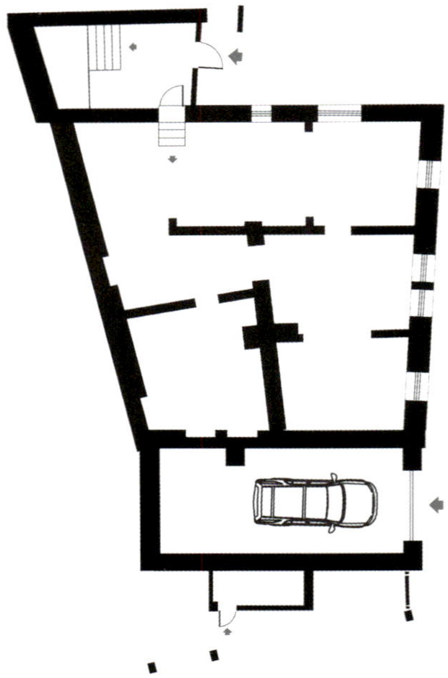

Ground-floor plan

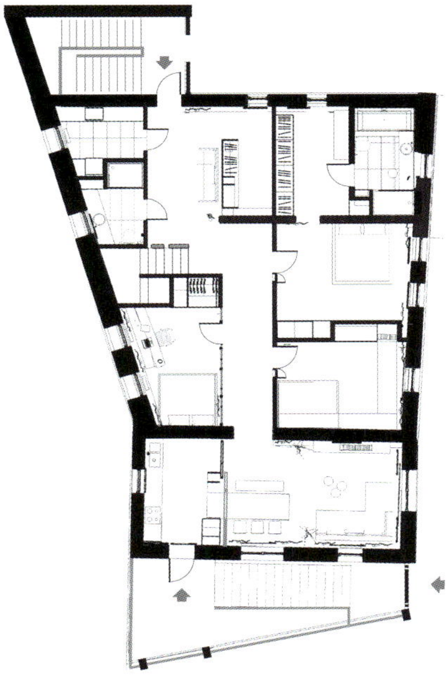

First-floor plan

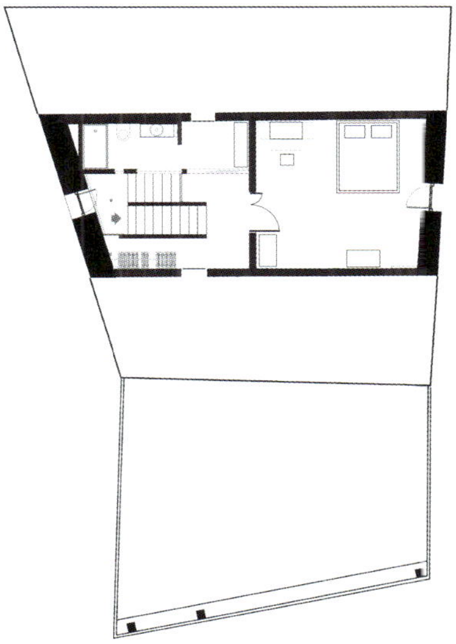

Second-floor plan

FITTY WUN

DESIGN: Feldman Architecture, Inc.
LOCATION: San Francisco, United States
AREA: 4,188 square feet (389 square meters)
COMPLETION YEAR: 2014
ORIGINAL BUILDING: 1915
PHOTOGRAPHY: Joe Fletcher

A family of five had shared a two-bedroom, one-bathroom house for many years before they were finally ready to transform the circa 1915 Marina-style house into their dream home with enough space to absorb the lively energy of their active and fun-loving family.

The clients desired a house focused on large, light-filled central spaces where the kids and friends of the family would love to hang out for many years to come. They also wanted a space that would act as "A welcoming, warm kind of Panopticon that allows the boys the freedom to be boys while the parents are strategically within ear-, if not always eyeshot, to arbitrate, adjudicate, and apply basic medical attention."

The completely reworked front facade is an interpretation of a traditional townhouse—a simple composition that blends in with the neighborhood but hints at the modern interior through scale, material choice, and updated details. In contrast, the modern composition of the rear facade more directly reflects the modern sensibility of the interior architecture with large apertures to bring in light and form a connection to the rear yard. The newly excavated sunken courtyard provides both the physical connection and natural light to the bedroom and the family room located in the basement level.

The main floor consists of an open-plan kitchen, dining, and living rooms. The kitchen opens upward to the ceiling, bringing light down from two stories above. Nooks and innovative storage solutions allow the three connected rooms—used for cooking, eating, working, and playing—to be the hub of the household without clutter. The living room flows out onto a deck and into the backyard, where there is plenty of space for the family's varied, energetic activities.

The metal-screened stair, backed by a tiled feature wall, leads from the street-level entry to the upper floors, where a catwalk connects the bedrooms and rings the atrium. The master suite is located along the rear of the upper level with floor-to-ceiling window providing a strong visual connection to the rear yard. The children's bedrooms are located across the open atrium, providing just the right amount of separation, but still within eyeshot of the parents,

rather than down a long and narrow hallway as is often the case in the typical urban townhouse floor layout. The relatively compact footprint of the children's bedrooms are compensated with extra ceiling volume. Small loft areas take advantage of the verticality of the space and connect the two bedrooms via a hidden passage door for the kids to crawl across.

A diagonal stair over the atrium leads up further to a floating office 'pod' and the roof deck. The pod provides an acoustically separated space for family members to occasionally escape from all the excitement below. The design of the pod door serves as a counterpoint to the clean lines of the fiber-cement-board-clad pod and the industrial aesthetics of the steel staircase with more traditional detailing and hand-stenciled sign reflecting the clients' senses of humor. The roof deck, one of the best spots in the neighborhood to catch the group of local parrots putting on their daily show, is surrounded by a green roof and looks out to broad views above the neighboring buildings.

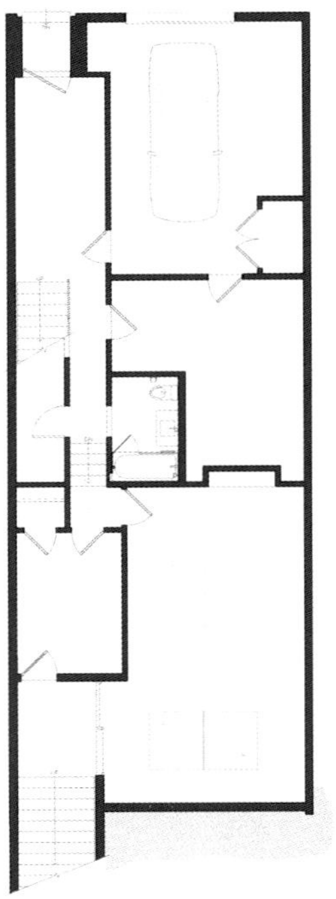

Ground-floor plan

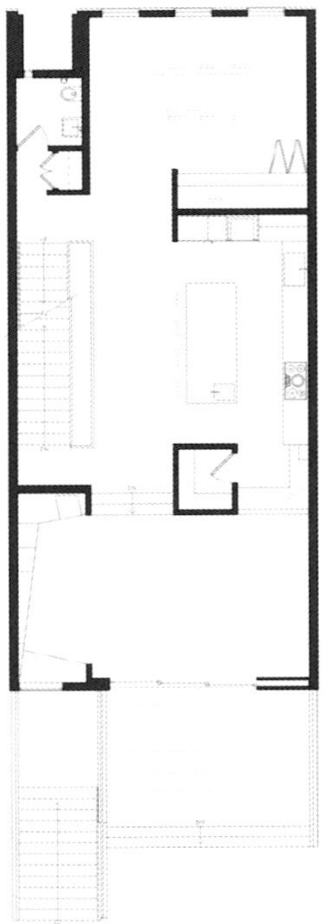

First-floor plan

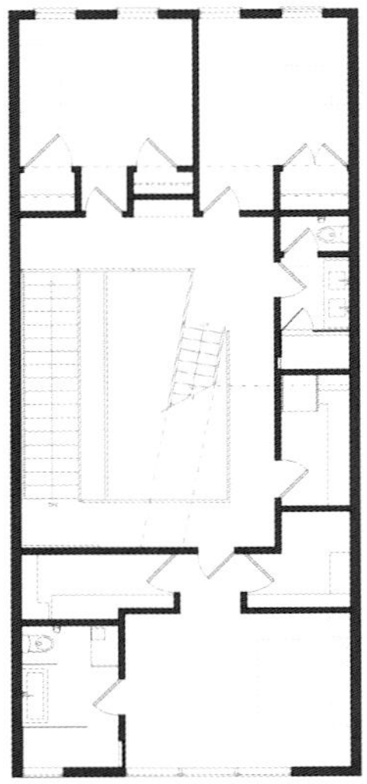

Second-floor plan

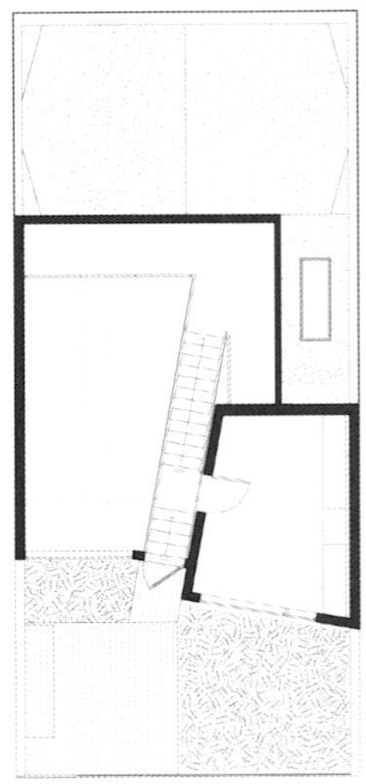

Pod and roof plan

CASA TMOLO

Before its conversion, the farmhouse was untouched for over five decades and needed a complete renovation to be adapted for contemporary needs. There were two construction sites: the main house and a stable. The main house was in a very bad condition, overgrown with vegetation, and numerous repairs had to be made to make it livable. The stone and timber structure of the stable had significantly deteriorated and most of the walls had to be replaced.

The position and materiality of the architecture was maintained, although given the farm's crumbling state, the new facade of the main house was reconstructed with white concrete and local stone.

In the main house, an insulating lining forms the new load-bearing structure, reinforcing the old stone walls and providing thermal insulation. The parts of the facade formerly of stone and brick weatherboarding were replaced by a monolithic wall of insulating concrete with formwork, which reproduces the former texture of the timber. Windows sit within deep recesses and can be screened behind large wooden shutters that reference the style of stable doors.

DESIGN: PYO arquitectos
LOCATION: Asturias, Spain
AREA: 4,456 square feet (414 square meters)
COMPLETION YEAR: 2013
ORIGINAL BUILDING: 1960s
PHOTOGRAPHY: Miguel de Guzmán

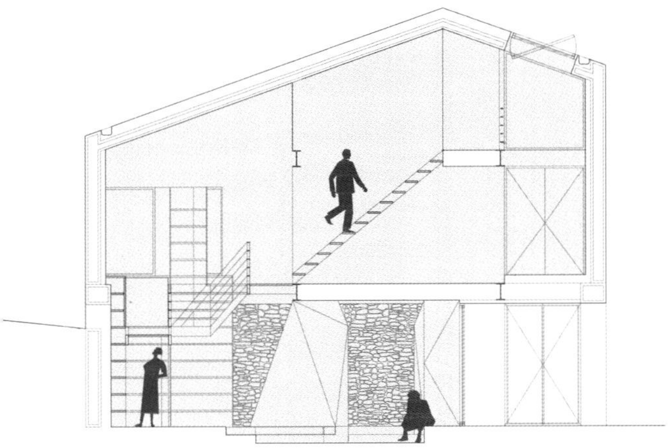

Cross section

Longitudinal section

Located on a steep south-facing mountain slope overlooking the valley, the main house clings to a site with a 6.5-foot (2-meter) difference in level between the north and the south facade. In harmony with the slope of the terrain, the staggered arrangement of the ground floor levels provides a sequence of connected spaces, avoiding conventional interior partitions. In the interior, supporting walls were replaced by light metal pillars, opening up a large triple-height living room along the entire length of the building, which allows daylight to enter. A generous metal staircase gives access to the different rooms of the house.

A mix of white concrete and iron beams coexist with well-worn stone, weather-beaten wood, and local stone. The interior space was organized around four diamond-shaped elements, which run vertically through the house: the four muses, main characters in this family holiday home that refer to the client's four daughters. On the first floor, two bedrooms were connected through a double-height space with views over the valley, leading to the main bedroom corner terrace.

In the stable, the haylofts on the upper floor were converted into bedrooms, freeing the space on the ground floor for a large central lounge that serves different purposes.

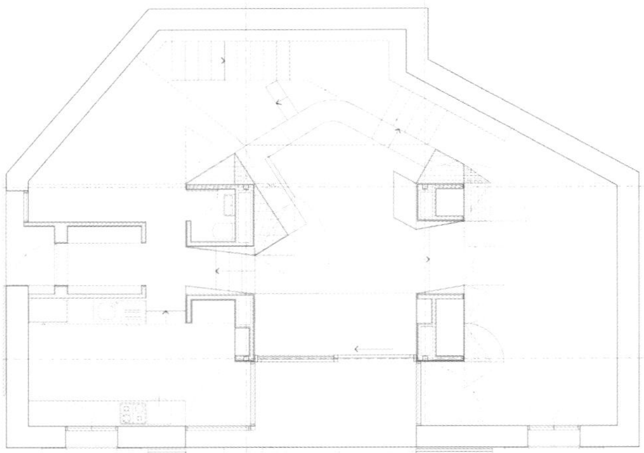

Ground-floor plan

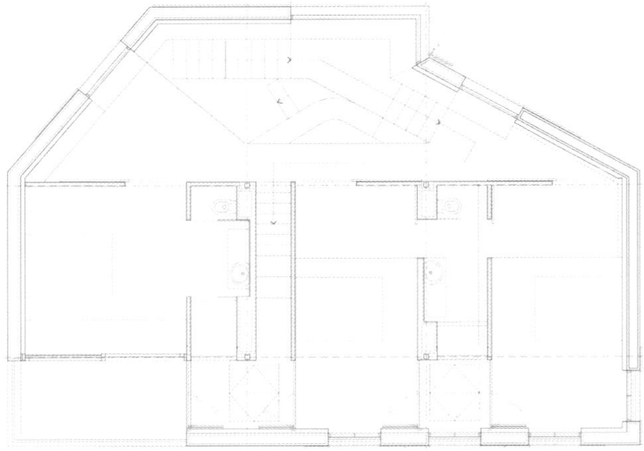

First-floor plan

PRODUCT OF COLOMBIA
70 kg NET

CHAPTER 4

TIMELESS TRANSFORMATION

BROOKLYN TOWNHOUSE

DESIGN: Takatina LLC
LOCATION: New York, United States
AREA: 2,350 square feet (218 square meters)
COMPLETION YEAR: 2018
ORIGINAL BUILDING: 1900
PHOTOGRAPHY: Mikiko Kikuyama

The three-story townhouse, built originally around 1900, was severely damaged in 2012 when superstorm Hurricane Sandy flooded the basement and ground floor with 8.5 feet (2.6 meters) of water. A portion of the building collapsed, requiring a complete gut renovation. Working closely with the New York City housing recovery program 'BUILD IT BACK,' this project became the first in the city to elevate an existing attached masonry row-house so that the ground floor would be 2 feet (500 centimeters) above the high-water line, the so-called Design Flood Elevation (DFE).

The main concept and name of this project emphasized the lifting of the building as a recognition of the process of destruction and recovery for a new set of environmental conditions. This design imperative led to the creation of the dramatic open loft space filled with natural light that merged the exterior and interior space in an extended, raised garden, designed by Urban Green. Flood-resilient design guidelines were incorporated throughout and all the floor elevations were also raised as a result of locating the first floor above the DFE. Meeting the new code requirements enabled the overall height of the building to be increased, accommodating the new penthouse addition.

The ground floor living quarters enjoy a dramatic 17-foot (5-meter) double-height space with monumental glazing to blur the boundary between the inside and outside. It opens to the south rear garden through the restored deck. The mezzanine and the floor below have a more domestic atmosphere with a modest ceiling height and comprise the master bedroom, children's bedroom and bathroom. The mezzanine utilizes a custom blackened cable net designed by Czech company Cabletech in Prague, the owners' original home, to minimize the separation between the spaces and create a more impressive view out the back wall to the garden.

The same design concept was applied to the top two floors to create a two-bedroom rental unit. The penthouse has an open living space quarter with large sliding doors that open to the rooftop terrace garden and panoramic city view, while the second floor houses intimate private quarters.

BMB

The new custom patterned aluminum shingle wraps the entire penthouse and bulkhead volume creating a striking 'box on a box' with subtle sparkling effects when hit with natural light during the day. The juxtaposition of the existing exterior brick facade and new metal penthouse creates an iconic contrasting presence on the street, reinforcing the newly elevated design of the structure.

Public circulation was placed to the west side with a monumental narrow stair as often found in classic loft buildings. A dramatic double-height entrance door with frosted wire glass also indicates the elevation of the entire house while bringing diffused light into the space and enhancing the unique front step material change from concrete and tile to wood per the flood design guidelines.

For the interior finish, the fully reclaimed and rebuilt brick wall is featured with exposed steel reinforcement and sections of newly painted insulated walls as a carefully studied the composition. The interior palette of white walls, polished concrete floor, and brick creates a calm background for warm vintage wood furnishing, a large collection of philosophy, art and architecture books, and a beautiful mix of interior plantings that echoes the exterior garden.

Penthouse plan

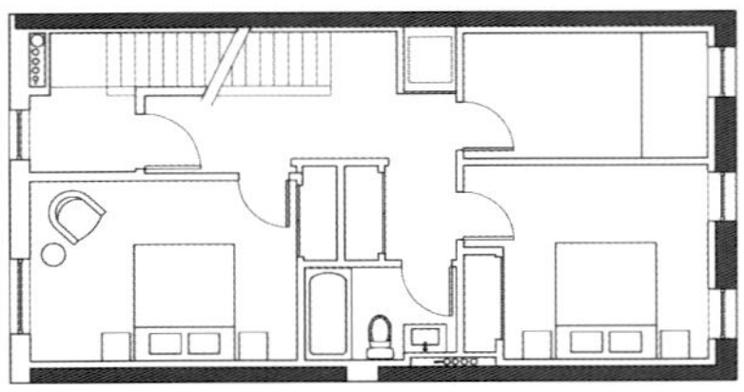

First-floor plan

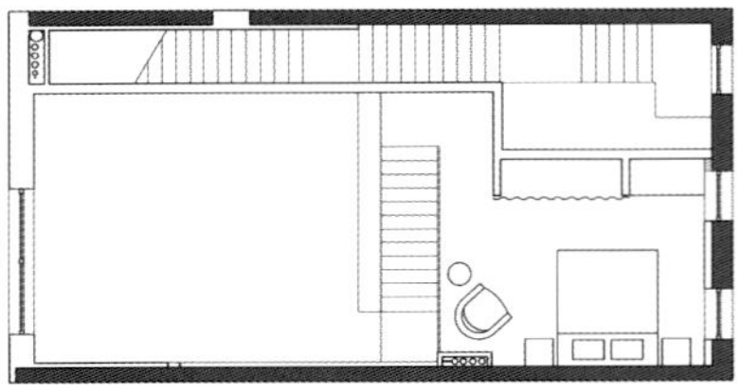

Mezzanine floor plan

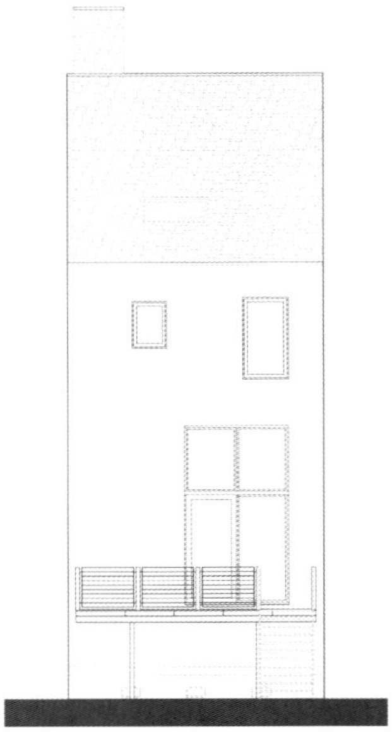

Elevation

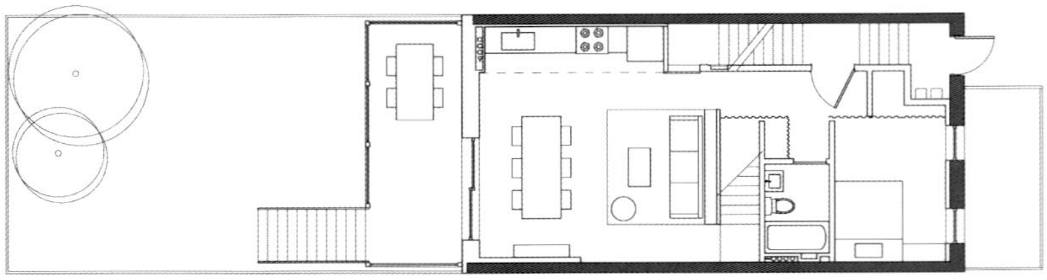

Ground-floor plan

SHIMOTOYAMA HOUSE

A young couple with children purchased an original 53-year-old Japanese house surrounded by country landscape with the intention of renovating it to suit their requirements.

The design team hoped to harmonize the balance between the timeless original elements of the residence with a fresh, modern aesthetic, interconnecting the spaces in the middle. Using the original materials, they endeavored to not make too many changes.

The flooring material was specially designed in ash and Bordeaux pine, which was among the original materials. The ceiling used Lauan plywood, which also adapted to the original building.

Removing the expanded and renovated parts of the building, which had been installed in the years since original construction, the designer reinstated the original rice-field character, inserting new elements from there. The original Japanese-style room was made into a garden, and the edge side was made to be outside, adding external factors and creating a comfort of the space where various elements were interwoven. The rich space was created by externalizing the interiors and inserting new elements while retaining some of the original features.

Expanding the volume to the minimum necessary for living space, the designer inserted external factors to allow for natural light and air flow. Originally, the interior and exterior of the house were divided by walls and windows. However, the designers were able to connect the outside and the inside more gently with enlarged windows, glass doors, and a central void to create a light-filled comfortable space where natural light flows and air circulates.

DESIGN: ALTS Design Office
LOCATION: Shimotoyama Ritto, Japan
AREA: 2,799 square feet (260 square meters)
COMPLETION YEAR: 2018
ORIGINAL BUILDING: 1965
PHOTOGRAPHY: Kenta Kawamura

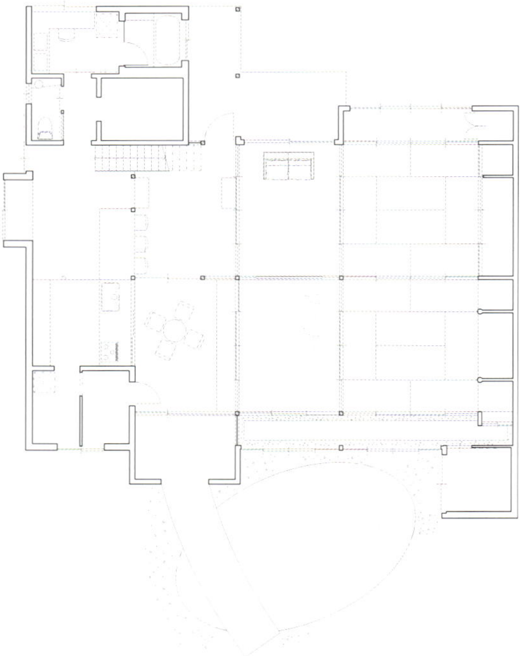

Ground-floor plan

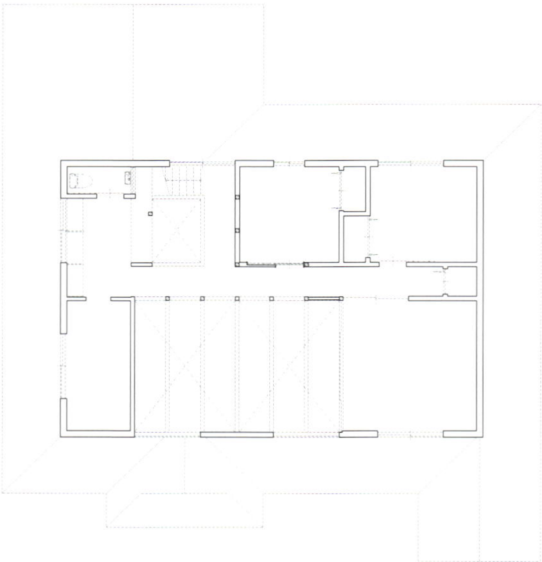

First-floor plan

3SHOEBOX HOUSE

Located within the city center of Ljubljana, Slovenia, this renovation transformed the 1934 small house that originally stood on the site.

The original home was designed by architect Emil Navinsek, known for his innovative concepts of spaces in architecture. He designed this house next to his own residence for his two unmarried elderly sisters. The street now consists of typically one-family houses mostly built in the 1960s and 1970s with a combination of white plaster render and dark wood cladding.

The extension was created by constructing different intersections between the old and the new part on each floor. It is composed of three cube volumes, each in a proportion of a shoebox like existing house floorplan. The boxes are stacked with 90-degree shifts creating overhangs and terraces. The volumes are clad in dark wood—spruce vertical lattice—in the context of the surrounding street architecture.

The structure is a combination of a concrete base, metal frames, and wooden substructure. Interior of the new part is formed mostly by wall cladding creating integrated wardrobes and walls. The old house is simply renovated keeping all the existing textures and materials.

The interior of the original old house and the new extension are connected in different layouts. The new extension pierces through old walls creating new volumes: the ground floor is now a living area, the children's rooms are on the first floor as well as a guest room, and the top floor contains the master bedroom.

The heart of the house, and the intersection of both volumes and also the connection of old and new, is a staircase attached to a main vertical concrete wall. Inspired by Adolf Loos, the interior forms include elevated podiums, niches, wardrobes, small sitting areas, and is partly extended into small spaces in the existing part of the house creating private living areas on each floor.

DESIGN: OFIS Architects
LOCATION: Ljubljana, Slovenia
AREA: 2,454 square feet (228 square meters)
COMPLETION YEAR: 2017
ORIGINAL BUILDING: 1934
PHOTOGRAPHY: Tomaz Gregoric

Ground-floor plan

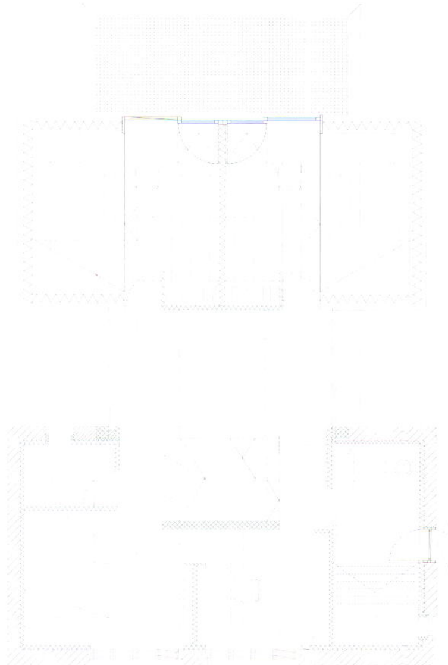

First-floor plan

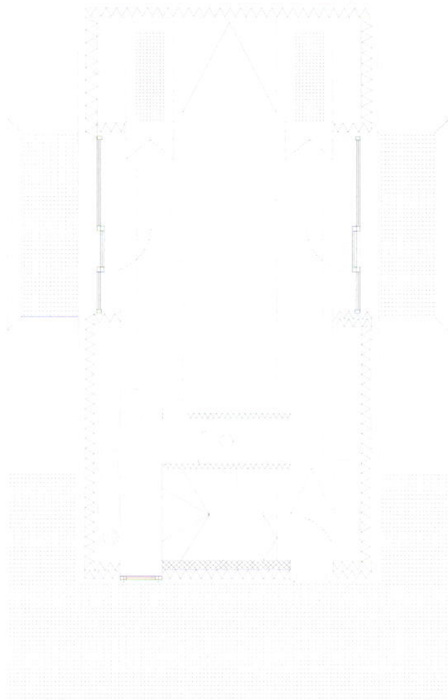

Second-floor plan

GITARREN HAUS

Perched on a steep block with majestic harbor views, the clarity of this original Australian postwar cottage had been muddled by decades of ad-hoc alterations. Built on a bushland site in 1951 by a local businessman, the dwelling is located within Walter Burley Griffin's Castlecrag development, where new roads were laid out to follow the contours of the peninsula, resulting in house allotments straddling curving roads and sitting atop rocky ledges.

Given the steep topography, the owner's brief was to rethink and rearticulate the flow of the whole home by substantially improving the ground floor level plan and creating a renewed lower ground-floor level rumpus/music room and cellar.

The dwelling had become dilapidated and dark in parts due to the poor quality of construction and materials used in the additions and alterations made by previous owners. As a result, the current owners sought not only a thorough refurbishment of the dwelling, but also desired a light-filled home with excellent indoor/outdoor flows to the entertaining deck, garden, and pool—necessary actions to bring close the magnificent bushland views and vistas of Sydney's Sailors Bay. Accessed via a steep winding set of stone steps, the owners wanted the house to be "worth it" and comfortable when one arrived from the trek up the hill.

As Castlecrag is now largely a heritage conservation area, characterized by the sandstone and masonry dwellings built to Burley Griffin's covenant for the suburb, it was important that the Gitarren Haus celebrated and improved the expression of the existing dwelling and its original masonry construction. Inspired by the setting and the elemental period qualities of the original dwelling, the significant sandstone base and arches were refurbished and highlighted to provide a clear reference to the many other Castlecrag homes and sites with sandstone elements, including those by Burley Griffin.

DESIGN: Bijl Architecture
LOCATION: Sydney, Australia
AREA: 3,068 square feet (285 square meters)
COMPLETION YEAR: 2017
ORIGINAL BUILDING: 1951
PHOTOGRAPHY: Katherine Lu

Reason within the Bounds of Religi
TIM WINTON
The Elegant Cockroach
PORTRAITS
John Berger on Artists
AYN RAND

The Austerity-era character of the brick volume was cleaned up with a minimalist approach to color and by simplifying the material language, so that the existing substantial sandstone lower ground floor and rear volume could be refurbished and brought back to life. This included streamlining the fenestration, which had previously been very fussy and in poor condition, and consolidating the awkwardly shaped deck, which offered expansive views that were not maximized in the previous arrangement of the dwelling's key spaces. This was softened externally by the stained-timber eaves, an obvious contemporary touch, providing a naturalistic warmth to the interface of the dwelling with the external spaces.

Intent on simplifying the interior scheme and opening up sight lines to the exterior, the layout and flow of the internal spaces was entirely reconsidered, all excess partitioning stripped back, the roof punctuated with deep skylight-wells. The family spaces were prioritized with large glazed sliding doors allowing the home to seamlessly segue onto the revitalized deck, looking out to the view and the subtropical garden surrounds.

By simplifying the dwelling, the humble structure began to take on real grandeur: from the hipped and tiled roof and the gentle sandstone arches to the manner in which the house nestles into its surrounds, while the inside was refreshed with its flow and purpose renewed.

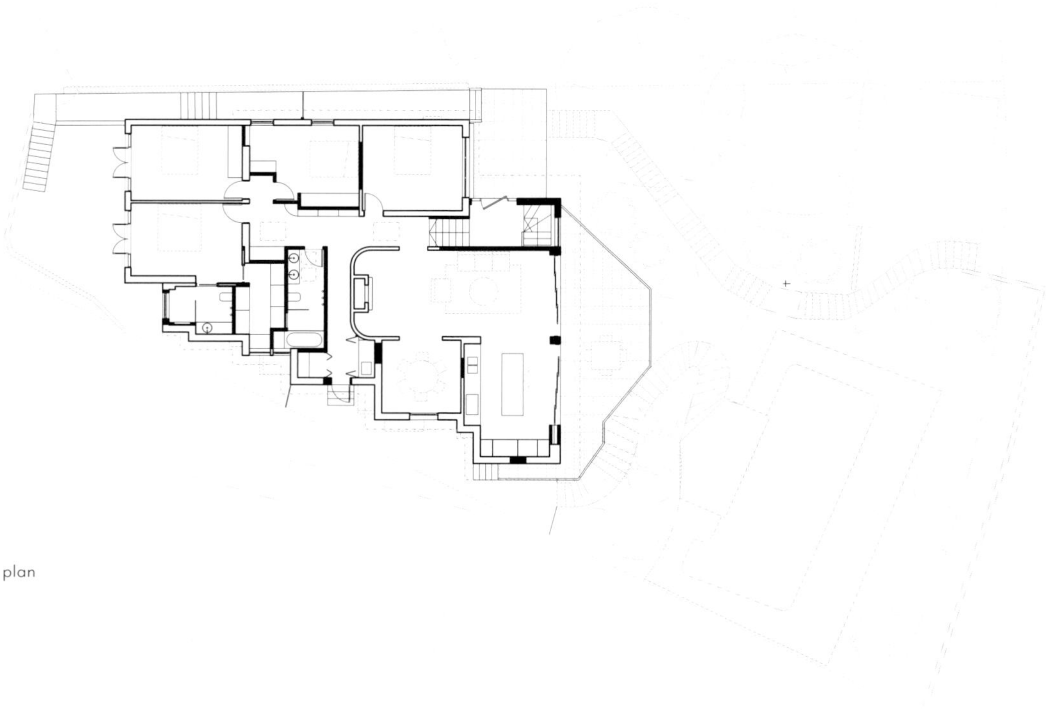

Ground-floor plan

JAZZ UP RESIDENCE

The property was built and owned by the City of Melbourne Building Society around 1889. The brief was to renovate and restore the existing main building, including the original outbuilding laundry, as well as extending the footprint of the non-original rear part. The kitchen was opened up to become part of a larger space that includes a dining area and a sitting area. They were also tasked with adding as much storage as possible. Soft gray built-ins were installed matching the kitchen cabinets, which help to unify the open room.

Joinery items formed a major part of the design in order to create generous storage areas in each bedroom. The designer created a floor-to-ceiling wardrobe in the bedroom as well as a library shelf unit in the spare room to house the client's substantial book collection.

The client was eventually convinced to continue the timber floor to the rear of the house instead of keeping the existing slate tiles in the rear and timber floorboards in the front of the house.

The existing internal plastered brick walls and the original ceiling including the ceiling roses and original cornices were fully restored. The internal walls including the new extension were given a fresh coat of paint in natural white to give a more contemporary feel and the new smoked oak timber floor provides warmth.

The rear part of the house was connected to the new garage through the existing rear courtyard. The studio also created an outdoor–indoor living area with an engineered-timber deck for entertaining.

The new light court along the southern boundary provides natural light and ventilation for the second bedroom/study as well as creating a visual connection to the rear courtyard through the new window in the kitchen. As the name of the project suggests, through design the studio was truly able to 'Jazz Up' this beautiful Victorian terrace.

DESIGN: SWG Studio
LOCATION: Melbourne, Australia
AREA: 1,270 square feet (118 square meters)
COMPLETION YEAR: 2017
ORIGINAL BUILDING: 1889
PHOTOGRAPHY: Sarah Anderson Photography

BIG SHED
HADID
SEPIA
NEW POSTER ART

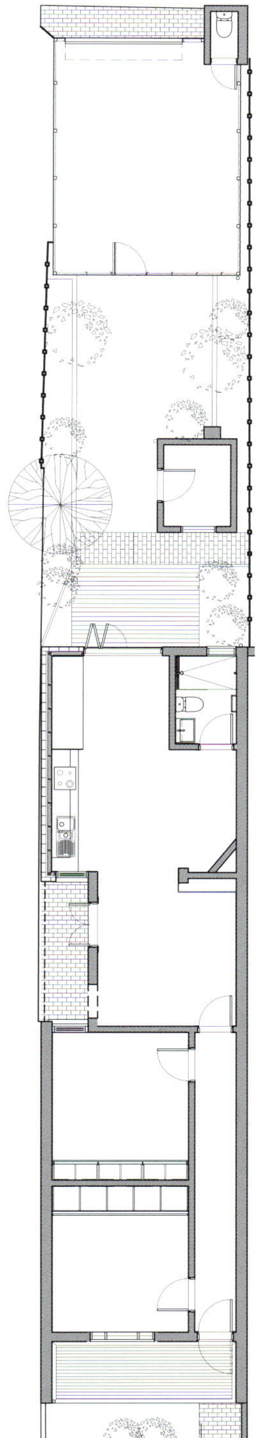

Floor plan

SPIDER HOUSE

This project involved an extension and renovation of a 1960s solid orange-brick suburban two-level house, involving a complete aesthetic renewal of the entire house. This was achieved with a series of infill additions, new veranda structure, reconfiguring some internal walls, and part deconstruction of the tiled hip roof to form a dramatic internal ceiling, as well as a complete renovation throughout.

The idea was to bring the solid but tired suburban brick house into the twenty-first century and redesign it to suit contemporary needs and standards, including passive solar design elements such as deep verandas, light-filled internal courtyards and study areas, as well as en suites and new additional bathrooms. A separate studio apartment on the lower level was also created, and the gardens excavated and landscaped to form private courtyards.

The project was a collaboration involving the architect, builder, and interior designer all contributing equally in all areas of design, including planning, layout, materials, and budget.

A few adventurous elements were explored with the white terrazzo flooring in the casual living areas as well as interesting ceiling forms and large areas of internal courtyard glazing creating a gallery effect within the house. The expansive areas of white finishes were tempered by the use of soft cedar timber paneling and trim.

The interior palette and materials were kept simple and consistent and also continued externally on the building reflecting the outside within, using cedar paneling ceilings, white terrazzo flooring, white walls and brickwork, and black-steel trim and window frames.

The existing heavy tiled hipped roof at the front was altered to form a windowed gable and to provide a dramatic ceiling within the living area below, bringing northerly light within to the kitchen area of the house. A veranda was added at the front to provide shade to the north and over the upper deck and entry, and to, in part, disguise the building's former life as a classic suburban modern brick and tiled house.

DESIGN: ITN Architects and Emma Dwyer
LOCATION: Melbourne, Australia
AREA: 2,476 square feet (250 square meters)
COMPLETION YEAR: 2017
ORIGINAL BUILDING: 1960s
PHOTOGRAPHY: Pru McMillan

18

ANITY FAIR 100 YEARS

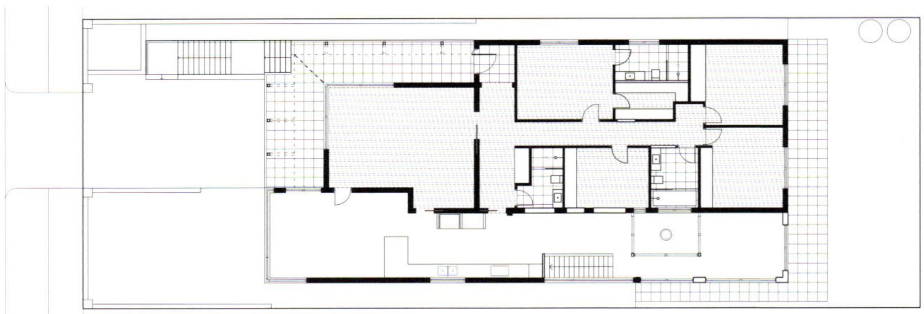

First-floor plan

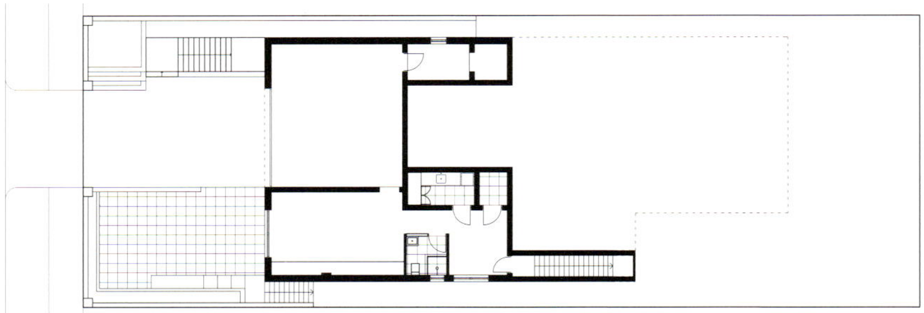

Ground-floor plan

ST VINCENTS PLACE RESIDENCE

As a modern renaissance home, the St Vincents Place Residence is a new archetype developed through reinterpretation of classical references with a modern sensibility. The client, as a patron, put his belief in architecture, artists, and artisans to create a nourishing environment that goes beyond surface treatments by inscribing contemplative experiences into the physical form.

Positioned behind a significant heritage facade, the new extension offers a cultural bridge between historical significance and modern progress. Embracing the consideration of time, the design response examined pinnacles of architecture and design throughout history. It recreated original elements that extract and expand upon qualities of substance, inspired by those that are proven to span the test of time. Although the majority of the home is a new building, it is not immediately recognizable as such.

The reworking of older-style details in the front section of the original building included curved cornices, arched doors, and custom steel fireplaces, which were not typical modern construction methodologies, but felt at ease within the Victorian frontage. Integral to the details was an authentic demonstration of an unusual level of craftsmanship. Even the smallest of details, like the hand-stained dovetail joints along the timber skirting, are deserving of a moment's reflection.

The modern counterpart in the rear extension uses in situ concrete, terrazzo-style stone floors, painted timber ceilings, and bluestone walling to create a point of difference from the front. Rejecting stark minimalism, the classical details were exchanged for rich textures continuing the hand-hewn character throughout the house.

Leading the way to intellectual discourse, the substantial art collection explores topics in philosophy, literature, religion, and even science. At moments, these are literally written into the walls, such as the three-story light-well built around the light work *Heaven Is A Place Where Nothing Ever Happens* by artist Nathan Coley and the niche installation of the wax sculpture *Romeu 'my deer'* by artist Berlinde De Bruyckere.

DESIGN: B.E Architecture
LOCATION: Melbourne, Australia
AREA: 8,072 square feet (750 square meters)
COMPLETION YEAR: 2017
ORIGINAL BUILDING: 1870
PHOTOGRAPHY: Derek Swalwell

As carefully curated as the art collection, the interiors for the house are an eclectic mix covering diverse cultural references across many eras. Many of the rooms were positioned around knowledge, encasing collections of books on expansive shelves and using them as a centerpiece within the custom coffee table in the living room.

A refined, casual aesthetic was created, incorporating unique vintage pieces sourced from Europe and Asia as a direct historic reference. Each piece adds to the dialogue of the space with exotic and interesting stories of when or where they are from or how they were created. Many of the pieces are one-of-a-kind designs by B.E Architecture, commissioned expressly for this project, pushing the artisanal character of the architectural detailing into the furniture.

The multidisciplinary designer team addressed all elements of lighting, interiors, and landscaping, including many custom-designed pieces of furniture. The design did not accept the limitations of a standard terraced house, but created new solutions to explore what was possible in the urban context. The team worked closely with the engineers to develop a commercial solution to support the existing house and allow the addition of the new basement.

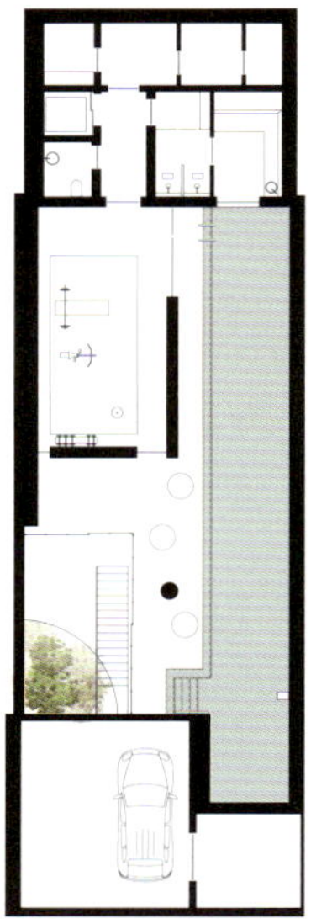

Basement floor plan

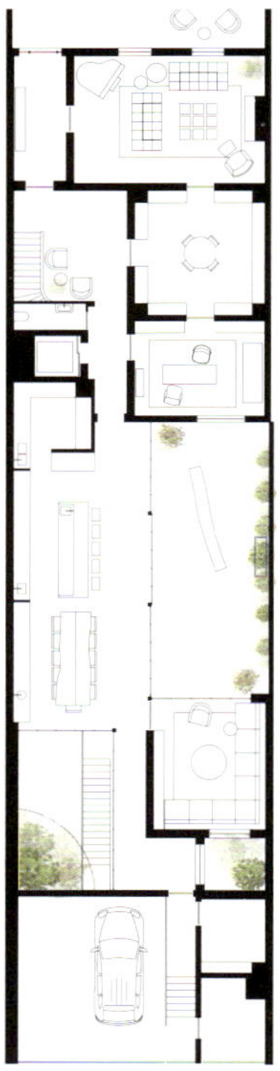

Ground-floor plan

First-floor plan

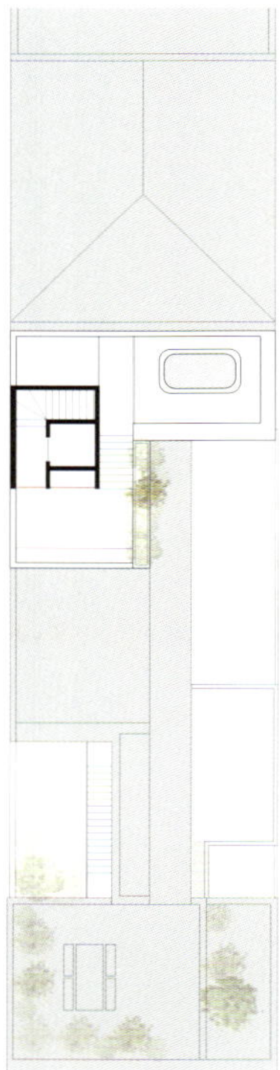

Roof plan

Harry Seidler
GILBERT & GEORGE
MNEMOSYNE
CCCP
ON THE ORIGIN OF ART
ART STUDIO AMER
ANSELM KIEFER
MIKE PARR THE TILTED
TACITA DEAN

BURT STREET RESIDENCE

The origins of this project came from modest beginnings. The clients wanted to add a secondary garage, a studio space, and upgrade their heritage-listed 1904 house. The architects saw significant opportunities and possibilities to reinvent how the clients were living and interacting on the site. The project soon evolved into a significant renovation and extension that utilized all of the site's endearing qualities.

Two previous extensions (1950s and 1980s) had choked the habitable spaces of natural light and any visual interaction with the backyard. To rectify this, the architects created new living spaces with skylights, light-wells, and a large expanse of the north-facing glass. 'The Curve,' as it became affectionately known, was a response to the unusual shape of the block, but it also helped to reorientate the space's northern aspect out toward the backyard. 'The Curve' wraps around the alfresco area, embracing the entertaining space while also creating privacy from adjoining properties.

The polished-concrete and black-steel details are unmistakably modern, but the addition of the softness of the honed marble and the rich tones from the timber help to soften the aesthetic. It creates a sympathetic but definite distinction from the old and new areas.

The extension offers a generous, light-filled space that centers on family interaction, entertaining the environment with the integration of indoor and outdoor spaces. With all the glass, skylights, and high ceilings, abundant light enters the house creating a beautiful effect. The aesthetic has a modern industrial vibe but with a touch of warmth and softness from the materiality and curved forms.

As the architects believe that a mock reproduction of heritage buildings is futile, there is a clear and defined contrast from the original part of the house. Each area holds architectural merit in its own right and its own era.

DESIGN: Keen Architecture
LOCATION: Fremantle, Australia
AREA: 5,059 square feet (470 square meters)
COMPLETION YEAR: 2016
ORIGINAL BUILDING: 1904
PHOTOGRAPHY: Dion Robeson

QUOTING SHAKESPEARE

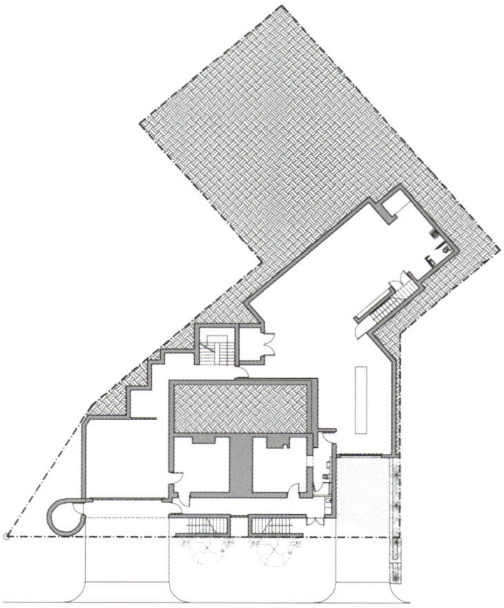

Basement floor plan

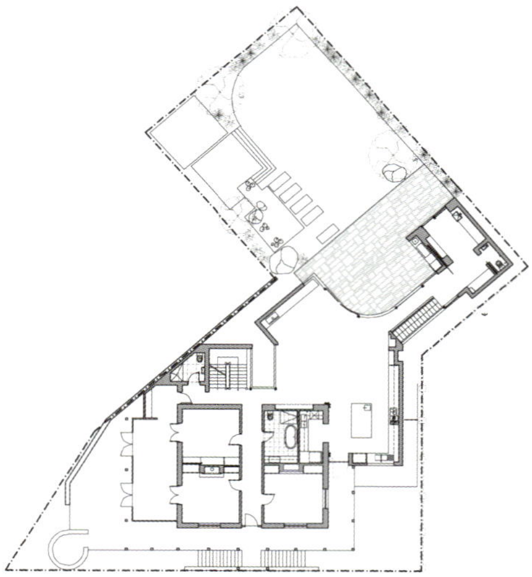

Ground-floor plan

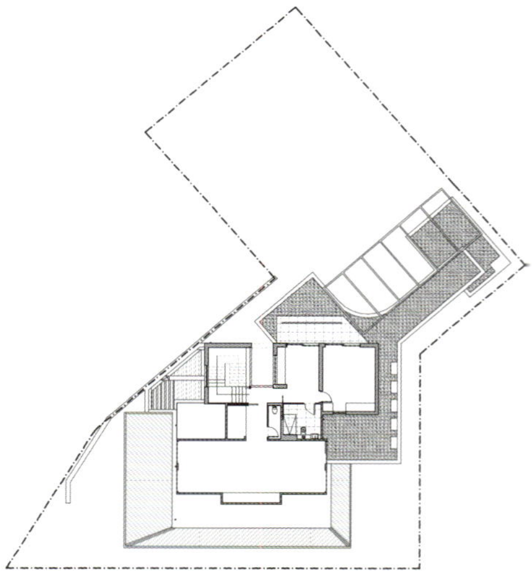

First-floor plan

FARMHOUSE UTRECHT

In the rural area near Utrecht, a large farmhouse was transformed into an exclusive house. An archetypal farm seems to be 'pierced' by a new wooden volume in the middle of the open countryside. With these interventions, the boundaries between inside and outside are shifted in various ways and the old building is energetically 'fed' by the new. What makes this assignment special is the integral approach at all scale levels, from refined garden design to spatial interior and from high-quality detailing to a lofty energy ambition.

The plot of the former dairy farm was completely cleared of all outbuildings, large barns, and structures. All the additional functions desired for the house were incorporated into one added volume that emerges at right angles from the farm. The house, thus, freely stands in the countryside and provides a point of reference for an interesting interplay between the interior and exterior. Boundaries between inside and outside were shifted, softened, reversed, or completely eliminated. Functionality, orientation, and perception were used as tools to shape the new transitions.

The new volume cuts through the farm at the location of the former fire wall (separation between the house and the stable). The tension between the old farm and the new volume created opportunities for special interventions and resolved functional issues. The clear new volume also reinforced the farm in its archetypal manifestation.

The spatial structure and basic principles were the basis for further detailing and the choice for individual furnishing elements and lighting. From the basic materials of wood, concrete, and steel, a rich variety of subtly different atmospheres was created through further refinement. Crystal clear choices in materials and details go hand in hand with separate 'found' pieces of furniture or eclectic lighting elements. A diverse atmosphere was created in each room, without losing the visual cohesion of the whole. A choice was often made for very basic materials such as stone or oak.

DESIGN: Zecc Architecten BV in collaboration with ZW6 | Studio Jeroen van Zwetselaar (for the interior & styling)
LOCATION: Utrecht, The Netherlands
AREA: 10,225 square feet (950 square meters)
COMPLETION YEAR: 2016
ORIGINAL BUILDING: 1929
PHOTOGRAPHY: Stijn Stijl Photography

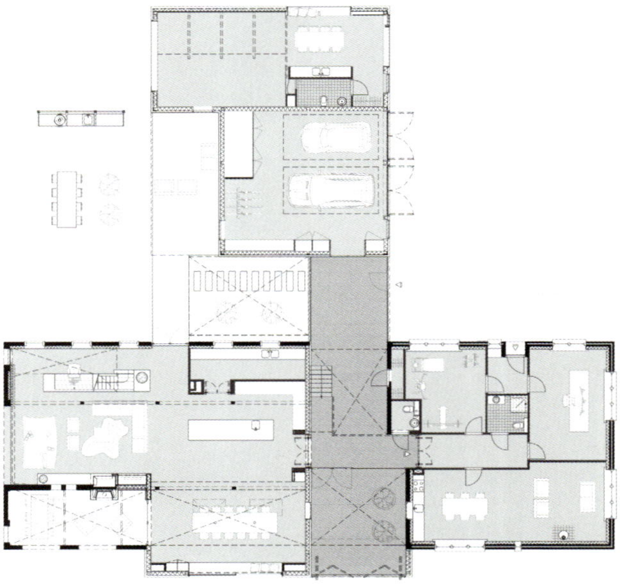

Ground-floor plan

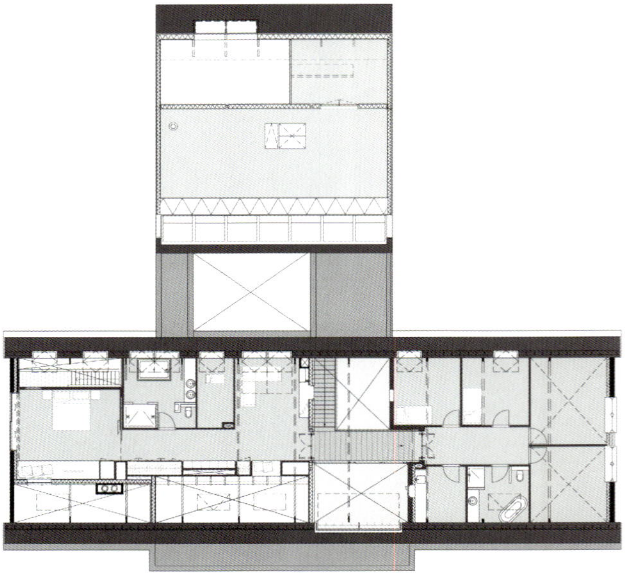

First-floor plan

VALENCIA HOUSE

DESIGN: DG Arquitecto Valencia: Isabel Roger Sánchez + Daniel González López
LOCATION: Valencia, Spain
AREA: 1,292 square feet (120 square meters)
COMPLETION YEAR: 2016
ORIGINAL BUILDING: 1916
PHOTOGRAPHY: Mariela Apollonio

Reinvented from an old townhouse with 100 years of history located in a town near Valencia, a young couple with a three-year-old daughter wanted to recover the family home that had deteriorated over the years, while retaining the small backyard and brick facade.

The existing distribution consisted of a series of small spaces without lighting or ventilation; thus, one of the big challenges was to get a new updated distribution, and a more open and functional feel.

The new layout of the house came as a result of introducing these elements into the project, while preserving the essence of the original building, and opening the main spaces to the backyard, which was felt to be the most important space in the house.

The original structure of wooden beams and beam fills, turned into an important part of the new layout as well as the old wooden doors that, although being in a new position, were all restored and reused to delimit the new spaces.

Located back in the house, there are the living spaces—the living room, kitchen, and the main room—with the backyard becoming the key area of the house, being a direct extension of the interior spaces.

The new layout of the house and the backyard were proposed in three areas: the central area where the most important rooms of the house were located; the entrance, hallway, and the big living room, where one of the characteristic elements of this type of housing, the fireplace, was located; and the dining room and the orchard area, a space where homeowners can enjoy growing their own vegetables and fruits.

In the upper area, where the rooms were located, two smaller rooms lighted up with the house's access road: the big master bedroom with a dressing, reading area and fireplace; and the pool area with the sunbathing and shower areas. Located in the lower area were the kitchen, with a little breakfast area, laundry, and a small barbecue with outdoor dining area.

17
17-1
17-B

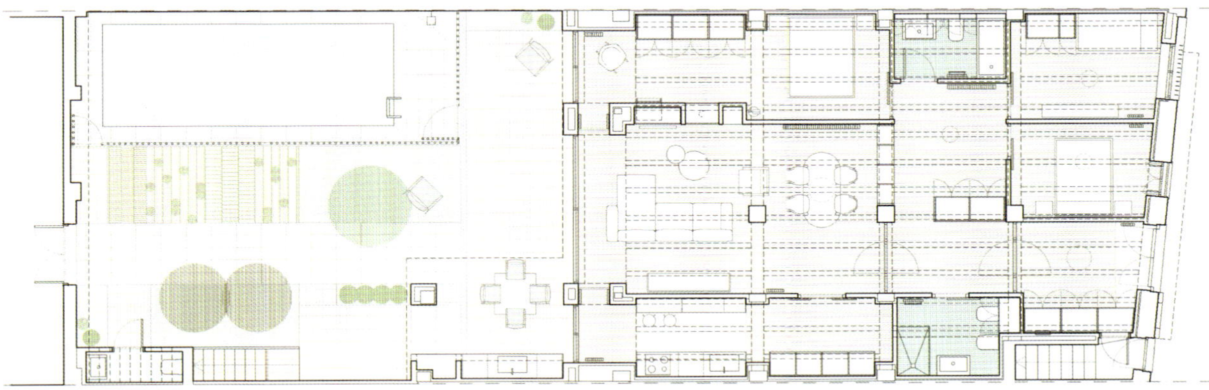

Ground-floor plan

PROJECT CREDITS

King Bill 14–23
Austin Maynard Architects || maynardarchitects.com

La Serena 24–31
David James Architects & Partners Ltd || davidjamesarchitects.co.uk

Laurelhurst Midcentury 32–37
mw|works || mwworks.com

Hibou House 38–43
Barbora Vokac Taylor Architect Inc. || bvtarchitect.com

House W 44–51
KC Design Studio || kcstudio.com.tw

Stealth House 52–59
MCK Architecture & Interiors || mckarchitects.com

23 Terrace 60–65
DRTAN LM Architect || dtlm.com.my

Kingswood 66–73
MC Architecture Studio || mcarchstudio.nz

Bold House 74–81
Personal Architecture || personal-architecture.nl

Renier Chalon 84–89
MAMOUT architectes and Atelier d'architecture AUXAU || mamout.be || auxau.com

Foster Road Retreat 90–97
Neumann Monson Architects || neumannmonson.com

Yellow+Terrazzo 98–103
Francesca Perani Enterprise and Bloomscape Architecture || francescaperani.com || bloomscape.org

Villa CC 104–9
Matteo Foresti Architecture Studio AB || matteoforesti.com

House Along Saigoku Highway 110–15
Koyori || koyori-n2.com

Residence Maribou 116–21
Alain Carle Architecte || alaincarle.ca

Casa VI 122–27
Alfredo Vanotti Architetto, EV+A lab Atelier d'Architettura & Interior Design || alfredovanottiarchitetto.it

Ichijoji House 128–33
atelier Luke || atelierluke.com

Lake Forest Park House 134–41
FINNE Architects || finne.com

A White House 144–51
RIGI DESIGN || rigi-design.com

Atelier 142 152–59
Atelier WILDA || wilda.fr

The Boundaryless House 160–69
Inspiration Group || gzins.com

Clifton Hill House 2 170–75
ITN Architects || itnarchitects.com

GC House 176–83
Iñaki Leite architect || inakileite.com

Waterline House 184–89
Ryntovt Design || ryntovt.com

Fitty Wun 192–97
Feldman Architecture, Inc. || feldmanarchitecture.com

Casa Tmolo 198–205
PYO arquitectos || pyoarquitectos.com

Brooklyn Townhouse 208–13
Takatina LLC || takatina.com

Shimotoyama House 214–21
ALTS Design Office || alts-design.com

3Shoebox House 222–27
OFIS Architects || ofis.si

Gitarren Haus 228–35
Bijl Architecture || bijlarchitecture.com.au

Jazz Up Residence 236–41
SWG Studio || swgstudio.com.au

Spider House 242–47
ITN Architects and Emma Dwyer || itnarchitects.com

St Vincents Place Residence 248–55
B.E. Architecture || bearchitecture.com

Burt Street Residence 256–63
Keen Architecture || keenarchitecture.com.au

Farmhouse Utrecht 264–71
Zecc Architecten BV || zecc.nl

Valencia House 272–77
DG Arquitecto Valencia || dgarquitecto.blogspot.com

Published in Australia in 2019 by
The Images Publishing Group Pty Ltd
ABN 89 059 734 431

Offices

Melbourne
6 Bastow Place
Mulgrave, Victoria 3170
Australia
Tel: +61 3 9561 5544

New York
6 West 18th Street 4B
New York, NY 10011
United States
Tel: +1 212 645 1111

Shanghai
6F, Building C, 838 Guangji Road
Hongkou District, Shanghai 200434
China
Tel: +86 021 31260822

books@imagespublishing.com
www.imagespublishing.com

The Images Publishing Group Reference Number: 1523

All photography is attributed in the Project Credits on page 278, unless otherwise noted. Front cover: Raphael Thibodeau (Alain Carle Architecte, Residence Maribou); Back cover (L–R): Guy-Joël Ollivier (MAMOUT architectes, Renier Chalon); David Foessel (Atelier WILDA, Atelier 142); Derek Swalwell (Austin Maynard Architects, King Bill); Stijn Stihl Photography (Zecc Architecten BV, Farmhouse Utrecht); Miguel de Guzmán (PYO arquitectos, Casa Tmolo); Page 2: Stijn Stihl Photography (Zecc Architecten BV, Farmhouse Utrecht); page 279: Tomaz Gregoric (OFIS Architects, 3Shoebox House). All of the 'before' imagery throughout this book has been supplied courtesy of the architect or design firm.

This book follows American spellings and usage throughout with an exception: floor-plan labels refer to ground floor in lieu of first floor.

NATIONAL LIBRARY OF AUSTRALIA

A catalogue record for this book is available from the National Library of Australia

Title: Building Character: Transforming Old Homes for Modern Living
Author: Santoso Budiman and Caleb Skene [Introductory texts]
ISBN: 9781864708363

Printed by Everbest Printing Investment Limited, in Hong Kong/China

IMAGES has included on its website a page for special notices in relation to this and its other publications. Please visit www.imagespublishing.com

Every effort has been made to trace the original source of copyright material contained in this book. The publishers would be pleased to hear from copyright holders to rectify any errors or omissions.